An Annotated Bibliography of Jazz Fiction and Jazz Fiction Criticism

Recent Titles in
Bibliographies and Indexes in World Literature

Modern Verse Drama in English: An Annotated Bibliography
Kayla McKinney Wiggins, compiler

Children's Books on Ancient Greek and Roman Mythology
Antoinette Brazouski and Mary J. Klatt, compilers

The Proverbial Bernard Shaw: An Index to Proverbs in the Works of
George Bernard Shaw
George B. Bryan and Wolfgang Mieder, compilers

Bibliographic Guide to Gabriel García Márquez, 1986–1992
Nelly Sfeir de González, compiler

The Juvenile Novels of World War II: An Annotated Bibliography
Desmond Taylor

The Spanish Civil War in Literature, Film, and Art: An
International Bibliography of Secondary Literature
Peter Monteath, compiler

Africa in Literature for Children and Young Adults: An Annotated
Bibliography of English-Language Books
Meena Khorana

Indigenous Literature of Oceania: A Survey of Criticism and
Interpretation
Nicholas J. Goetzfridt

Boccaccio in English: A Bibliography of Editions, Adaptations,
and Criticism
F. S. Stych

Cloak and Dagger Fiction: An Annotated Guide to Spy Thrillers
Myron J. Smith, Jr. and Terry White

Literature for Children and Young Adults about Oceania:
Analysis and Annotated Bibliography with Additional Readings for Adults
Mary C. Austin and Esther C. Jenkins

The Contemporary Spanish Novel: An Annotated, Critical
Bibliography, 1936–1994
Samuel Amell

An Annotated Bibliography of Jazz Fiction and Jazz Fiction Criticism

Compiled by
RICHARD N. ALBERT

Bibliographies and Indexes in World Literature,
Number 52

GP

GREENWOOD PRESS
Westport, Connecticut • London

Library of Congress Cataloging-in-Publication Data

Albert, Richard N.
    An annotated bibliography of jazz fiction and jazz fiction
criticism / compiled by Richard N. Albert.
        p. cm. — (Bibliographies and indexes in world literature,
ISSN 0742–6801 ; no. 52)
    Includes bibliographical references and index.
    ISBN 0–313–28998–0 (alk.paper)
    1. Short story—Bibliography. 2. Jazz—Fiction—Bibliography.
3. Jazz musicians—Fiction—Bibliography. 4. Musical fiction—
Bibliography. I. Title. II. Series.
Z5917.S5A43   1996
[PN6120.95.J28]
016.80883'9357—dc20   96–8937

British Library Cataloguing in Publication Data is available.

Library of Congress Catalog Card Number: 96–8937
ISBN: 0–313–28998–0
ISSN: 0742–6801

First published in 1996

Greenwood Press, 88 Post Road West, Westport, CT 06881
An imprint of Greenwood Publishing Group, Inc.

Printed in the United States of America

∞™

The paper used in this book complies with the
Permanent Paper Standard issued by the National
Information Standards Organization (Z39.48–1984).

10 9 8 7 6 5 4 3 2 1

CONTENTS

PREFACE

I make no claim for this being an exhaustive bibliography. However, it is far more than what is generally referred to as a "selected" bibliography. I found as I worked on this over the last several years that I frequently was finding new items merely by chance. So it seems natural to assume that there are many more novels, short stories, and pieces of criticism that will eventually be uncovered.

Also, there may be differences of opinion over what should or should not be included. Not all will agree on what constitutes "jazz fiction," or whether the label is even appropriate. Certainly, arguments over whether there is what might be termed a "jazz genre" would be inappropriate. The intent of this bibliography is to acknowledge that jazz and blues, in varying degrees, have made their mark in fiction. Making choices is difficult. Nevertheless, this bibliography is intended as a starting point and probably should be regarded as a work in progress.

Thanks are due to the inter-library loan staff at Illinois State University's Milner Library, especially Helga Whitcomb, Sharon Wetzel, and Carol Ruyle, all of whom made major efforts to locate difficult-to-find materials. Thanks also to the English Department at Illinois State for released time to work on the bibliography and jazz related critical articles. Also, I am indebted to Ruth Faulkner for her help with proofreading and to Editor Laura Clark for her keen eye and fine advice. Finally, thanks to my wife Cathy for her love, encouragement, and patience as I searched, read, and annotated.

INTRODUCTION

About as much attention is being given to jazz today as there ever has been. The popularity of the compact disc (CD) and its capacity of seventy to eighty minutes of playing time has given rise to a large number of reissues of past jazz recordings, as well as new recordings by young, contemporary jazz performers, many of whom, such as the Marsalis brothers, are reviving an interest in the jazz heritage of the legends—Charlie Parker, John Coltrane, Thelonious Monk, Billie Holiday, Art Blakey, Dizzy Gillespie, and many others. This vitality of jazz is evident around the world.

Also, in the last seven years the public at large was exposed to jazz via five excellent films: Clint Eastwood's *Bird*, based on the life of Charlie Parker; Charlotte Zwerin's *Straight No Chaser*, a documentary about Thelonious Monk; Bertrand Tavernier's *'Round Midnight*, a French film starring Dexter Gordon; *Let's Get Lost*, a documentary about Chet Baker; and Robert Altman's about-to-be-released *Kansas City*. Further, admirable films appealing to jazz aficionados have become available on video cassette—documentaries on Art Pepper, Miles Davis, Louis Armstrong, Charlie Parker, Billie Holiday, and others.

Interest in jazz is also indicated by the publication of a large number of books and periodicals devoted to jazz. One need only look to scholarly and university presses and their jazz publications to realize that jazz is fertile ground for biographical and critical examinations of the history of jazz, the music itself, and its artists and their recordings. The shelves of some of the new "super" book stores are overflowing with both new jazz publications and a whole series of reprints of books that have become at least minor classics. Long-standing jazz magazines such as *Down Beat, Jazz Journal International, Jazz Times, Coda,* and *Jazz Hot* continue to thrive.

But my purpose here is to show that jazz has had a meaningful and significant impact on fiction. For example, James Baldwin, Langston Hughes,

John Clellon Holmes, Jack Kerouac, Malcolm Lowry, Claude McKay, John A. Williams, Donald Barthelme, Thomas Pynchon, Ralph Ellison, Rudolph Fisher, Shelby Foote, James Jones, Albert Murray, J. F. Powers, Josef Škvorecký, Terry Southern, Julio Cortázar, and Eudora Welty have been influenced by the music to the degree that it has had a meaningful effect on many of their works. Numerous others, less well-known, also have a jazz and blues connection. Even earlier on in our literary history we see importance attached to various strains of jazz, from ragtime in James Weldon Johnson's *Autobiography of an Ex-Coloured Man* (1928), to the blues in Claude McKay's *Home to Harlem* (1928), Langston Hughes' *Not Without Laughter* (1930), Rudolph Fisher's "Common Meter" (1930), and George Washington Lee's Beale Street stories in the 1940s. Also, in the mid-1930s and through the 1940s there was a series of swing and big band stories, including little known works such as Wyatt Rundell's *Jazz Band* (1935), Dale Curran's *Piano in the Band* (1940), Robert Paul Smith's *So It Doesn't Whistle* (1941), and Henry Steig's *Send Me Down* (1941), as well as Dorothy Baker's popular *Young Man With a Horn* (1938), based on the legendary Bix Beiderbecke.

Probably the most prolific periods for jazz-oriented works were the 1950s and 1960s, many being produced by Beat Generation writers and many giving prominence to Charlie "Bird" Parker, who has probably been more frequently implied and directly referred to in modern literature than any other jazz musician. He is the subject of innumerable poems and stories that present him as a rebel artist and an inspiration to the oppressed. To ignore jazz and to ignore Parker is to ignore a significant aspect of poetry and fiction. He was held in high regard by the Beat Generation; they loved jazz, especially bebop, and what John Clellon Holmes, Beat insider and chronicler, says about the Beats applies as well to jazz musicians such as Parker:

> Their almost-maniacal [sic] efforts to find new modes, new forms, new styles to go with their new material, their new vision, has kept their work not only relevant, but consequential. . . . History will sort it out. Perspective is the last turn of the wheel. (Knight and Knight 11)

Parker has, indeed, been relevant. To give greater emphasis to his impact, here is a brief outline of his appearance in fiction. It was the publication of John Clellon Holmes's *The Horn* (1958) that began the perpetuation of the legend of Charlie Parker as rebel, alienated jazz musician (even though Elliott Grennard's short story, "Sparrow's Last Jump," predates it). Edgar Pool, the central, titular character, is nicknamed "The Horn" and reflects both Lester Young and Charlie Parker. Holmes details Edgar's career from his early years as a seminal bopster to his tragic end, the victim of excessive alcohol, drugs, and women—a life very similar to Parker's.

Holmes emphasizes the artist's continual quest for truth by highlighting Edgar's desire to play that one solo, even that one note that will be "something no one can stand, it's so true . . ." (227). He never does, but when he dies, his friend, Cleo, says he will begin the legend by writing on the subway wall, "The Horn still blows" (242).

Though Holmes's *The Horn* is one of the best examples of the strong influence of jazz in the Beat Generation lifestyle and in their writings, Jack Kerouac's *On the Road* and *The Subterraneans* and Holmes's first novel, *Go*, though not "jazz novels," also have many references to jazz. Like Parker, the Beats demonstrated a love of freedom and individuality and reflected it in their lives and writings, often in conflict with the more conventional attitudes of the post-World War II literary establishment and general public. *The Horn*, therefore, also occupies an important place in post-World War II American literature as a clear proclamation of the Beat credo and provides a point of reference for all of those individualistic nineteenth-century writers (Poe, Whitman, Melville, Thoreau, Hawthorne, Twain, Dickinson) also referred to in *The Horn*, whose ideas the Beats echoed in their own lives and works.

Another jazz novel inspired by Parker is Ross Russell's *The Sound* (1961). Russell, producer of Parker's Dial recordings and author of the popular, highly-regarded biography of Parker, *Bird Lives!*, had an insider's knowledge of the bebop jazz scene. *The Sound* has many references to jazz musicians and styles and employs much of the jazz jargon of the time. But most important of all, Russell knew Bird. His central character is not a saxophonist, but a trumpet player named Red Travers who is nicknamed "The Sound." Nevertheless, the reader is reminded of Parker as Russell traces Red's career and gives us an excellent overview of the competition between the "new" jazz and "traditional" jazz through the 1940s and into the 1950s. He give us a good feel for what it was like to be at a jam session, a member of a band doing one-nighters, and the inevitable use of drugs. Russell's characterization of Red Travers strongly reflects his personal experiences with Parker.

In John A. Williams's *Night Song* (1961), Parker is Richie Stokes and is nicknamed "Eagle"—an obvious reference to Parker's "Bird." But the central character is really a white man, David Hillary, a former college teacher who must come to terms with his deep-seated racial prejudice. Though Eagle may not be the central character, he is of primary importance and Parker as his model is obvious. He is a talented, innovative bop saxophonist whose ultimate downfall is overindulgence, especially with drugs. He becomes "a tired-looking young man who [has] grown very old" (Williams 179). When he dies, the newspaper headlines proclaim, "BOP KING DIES OF ADDICTION," and he leaves behind "three or four wives, each of them with the proper credentials, each extremely attractive, . . . and each of them wanting the body for burial." Signs begin to appear: "Eagle Lives" and "The Eagle Still Soars" (Williams 209-10).

James Baldwin's short story, "Sonny's Blues" (1957), uses Parker as a contrast to Louis Armstrong. Here, Parker does not appear as a character, but as a point of reference—Sonny's idol. Sonny is a young, aspiring jazz pianist at odds with his older brother (the narrator) who knows almost nothing about jazz and can only think of Louis Armstrong when Sonny tells him he wants to play jazz. Sonny responds that Armstrong's music is "old-time, down home crap" (120) and that he admires "Bird," calling him "just one of the greatest jazz musicians alive" (121). The narrator, who has finished college and takes pride in being a math teacher, represents the conservative, the traditional—as Armstrong did to a degree in jazz (Armstrong initially hated bebop jazz). Sonny represents a break with tradition, as had Parker in his development and promotion of the new jazz, bebop. Sonny also mirrors Parker in that Sonny has gotten into trouble with drugs at a very early age, as had Parker. This threatens not only Sonny's life, but also the narrator's (so the older brother believes). So the Parker and Armstrong references are very important in this story.

Other short stories with impressive references to Parker are Elliott Grennard's "Sparrow's Last Jump" (1947), Tony Scott's "Destination K.C." (1960), and Julio Cortázar's "The Pursuer" (1960). Grennard's prize-winning short story was first published in *Harper's Magazine* in May, 1947. Grennard, musician, composer, lyricist, and journalist, was in attendance at producer Ross Russell's legendary Charlie Parker "Lover Man" recording session on July 29, 1946. At this time, Parker was in the midst of severe mental and physical debilitation. The night of the session, Parker was in exceptionally bad shape and had great difficulty playing. Russell was frustrated at his anticipated loss of about a thousand dollars worth of recording studio time. However, the session did produce what is regarded by some as a classic rendition of "Lover Man." In Grennard's story, Parker is known as "Sparrow" Jones, and at the end of the story the narrator observes, "Yeah, Sparrow's last recording would sure make a collector's item. One buck, plus tax, is cheap enough for a record of a guy going nuts" (Grennard 426).

Tony Scott, jazz clarinetist and a contemporary of Parker, was inspired to write the brief, three-page short story "Destination K.C." after Parker's death. The story is an exercise in irony. The reader is privy to the conversation of two railway employees, Spody and Joe. Spody envies the life of jazz musicians like Parker—the life style that contributed strongly to Parker's early death—and can't understand how Bird could be so irresponsible. He tells Joe about his having met Parker one time:

> "So Bird says, 'What kinda gig you got?' . . . so I told him . . .
> I'm down the Railway Express, an' he says, 'I'll be down to see
> you one day,' so he says, 'I got friends ev'rywhere,' so I told
> him, Bird, anytime you come by, I'll take care of you" (82).

The end of the story reveals that Spody and Joe are, unknowingly, loading Bird's casket on the train for its journey to Kansas City and "taking care of" him. Another aspect of the irony seen in the story is that Parker did not really wish to be buried in Kansas City.

Argentine Julio Cortázar's "The Pursuer" is dedicated "In memoriam Ch. P." Parker here is Johnny Carter and the time is the early 1950s. The location is Paris, and Johnny is fighting drugs and experiencing hallucinations involving time. He is not dependable and often irresponsible (not showing up for gigs, losing or pawning his horn), a reflection of Parker. The notorious "Lover Man" recording session becomes the "Amorous" recording session that produces two songs— "Amorous" and "Streptomycin." But "The Pursuer" refers to two people: Johnny, of course, but, more importantly to Bruno, jazz critic and Johnny's biographer. Perhaps Johnny's pursuit is something that all artists in a sense pursue—truth. Bruno, on the other hand, is pursuing his own selfish ends, which in this case are dependent on how well his book on Johnny sells. It is due out in a second edition, and he must grapple with Johnny's displeasure with the first edition. The story is long and much more involved and gives insights into the motivations of different kinds of artists.

Raymond Federman, in "remembering Charlie Parker or how to get it out of your system," a section of his book, *Take It or Leave It* (1976), refers to the famed "Lover Man" recording session and the song itself, which was really made even more famous by Billie Holiday. However, Federman has Parker in concert, rather than in the studio. This interlude in Federman's story is a panegyric to Parker in which the white narrator concedes the necessity of being black in order to be in the same league with the late forties' bopsters. He describes being with Parker at a jam session in Detroit after a Jazz at the Philharmonic concert and lending Bird his new tenor sax, whereupon Parker blows "A 45 MINUTE SOLO (on MY OLD FLAME) An Historical Moment!" (N. pag.)

William Melvin Kelley's novel, *A Drop of Patience* (1965), also has some allusions to Parker, even though Kelley's protagonist, Ludlow Washington, is a blind-from-birth black man. Though his role is that of one of the innovators of a new jazz mode in the 1940s (evidently the controversial bebop, with its attendant hipster jargon and style of dress), his playing a saxophone is only implied; Kelley says that he had "a great many jazz musicians in mind, ranging from Bessie Smith to Lester Young to Charlie Parker and, of course, Ray Charles, because he was blind" (Newquist 207). What Kelley seems most interested in proclaiming is the idea that we in society too often ignore or forget our artists, alienating them to the extent that they become confused about their own identities or places in society.

These more extended examples of Charlie Parker in fiction denote his legendary status and popularity. But jazz has entered into the works of many writers in less overt or extensive fashion. Hugh L. Smith, Jr.'s 1958 article,

"Jazz in the American Novel," a shortened version of Chapter V of his 1955 Ph.D. dissertation, *The Literary Manifestation of a Liberal Romanticism in American Jazz*, was one of the first articles to draw attention to this. Smith notes three trends in novelists' references to jazz: "a quantitative increase in jazz subject matter, a qualitative advancement in the accuracy of portrayal of the jazz world, and a consistently romantic treatment of jazz subject matter" (467). He then surveys writers as wide-ranging as Michael Arlen, F. Scott Fitzgerald, Carl Van Vechten, Du Bose Heyward, Thomas Wolfe, Chandler Brossard, Dorothy Baker, Dale Curran, Harold Sinclair, Eudora Welty, John Clellon Holmes, John O'Hara, Henry Miller, James Jones, J. D. Salinger, Evan Hunter, Bucklin Moon, and Ralph Ellison. Smith's dissertation makes a sound case for jazz's indebtedness to American literature for what he recognized at that time as "its growing national recognition as an art form" (iii). His main thesis is that "all genres of the literature of Jazz have adopted an attitude of Liberal Romanticism in their treatment of Jazz" (ii). Liberal Romanticism is characterized as having the Romantic elements of "an expressive individualism, an ideal standard for both art and behavior, a belief in art approaching an art-religion, a general nonconformity to the *status-quo*, and an element of anti-materialism," along with the Liberal qualities of "a firm belief in racial equality and brotherhood, a strong sense of humor with which to meet reality, a general attitude of anti-snobbery and informality, and an implied belief in the perfectibility of mankind" (ii-iii).

A number of mystery and science fiction writers also have used a jazz setting for their stories, often to very good effect. Malcolm Braly's *Shake Him Till He Rattles* (1963) is a detective story of the hard-boiled school that expresses a keen familiarity with the bebop style of music and its practitioners. A more recent example of the murder mystery with a strong jazz background is Harper Barnes's *Blue Monday* (1991), set in 1935 Kansas City. A number of other jazz-oriented mystery stories have appeared in *Ellery Queen Mystery Magazine* issues and anthologies. Among science fiction writers, one of the most knowledgeable in the area of jazz is Robert Tilley, his "Willie's Blues" and "Something Else" being interesting examples of how the jazz tradition can enter into what on first thought appears to be an incompatible genre.

Since jazz as music has become an international language, it is no surprise that jazz-inspired literature is to be found among authors outside the United States. Some of the best is that of the Czech Josef Škvorecký, who presently lives in Canada and is highly regarded among international authors. *The Bass Saxophone: Two Novellas* (1979), "Eine kleine Jazzmusik" (1969) and "The Bebop of Richard Kambala" (1985) are only three of his stories that show the influence of jazz on his writing. Robert Tilley, mentioned earlier, is an Englishman, as are Benny Green and John Wain, among others, which is not surprising since the British are great jazz enthusiasts. Authors of various other nationalities can be found in Chris Parker, ed. *B Flat, Bebop, Scat* (1986), an anthology of previously-unpublished jazz short stories and poetry.

Jazz also has its lighter side, sometimes produced by the language and dress peculiarities associated with it. Steve Allen uses bop jargon ("hip" expressions and words) of the 1950s to refashion well-known fairy tales in his *Bop Fables* (1955). Octavus Cohen's "Music Hath Charms" is a humorous piece about the "World's Most Greatest Colored Musician," a con man who can't blow a note. Langston Hughes's street-wise Jesse B. Semple provides humor in the classic "Bop" and "Jazz, Jive, and Jam." Leonard Feather, the preeminent jazz historian and critic, satirizes jazz by taking on the guise of one Professor Snotty McSiegel, self-acclaimed jazz authority who claims, among other things, to be the originator of jazz concerts and bebop. In similar style, Marshall Brickman satirizes a musicologist's interview of a 112-year-old blues legend in "What, Another Legend?" Donald Barthelme's "The King of Jazz" parodies the jam session, likening it to a cowboy shootout.

The abundance of creative works that have strong jazz inspiration is evident. Also, the number of critical studies of the use of jazz and blues in fiction and plays is quite impressive. But Gayl Jones, in her discussion of Amiri Baraka's short story, "The Screamers," expresses a broader view about the importance of jazz and blues on literature and what it should generate: "A study of jazz and the whole of American literature would be welcome—one which compares and contrasts the uses of the music in the works of both African-American and European artists" (120).

Jason Berry concurs: "It's time to expand traditional notions of literary classification and broaden the boundaries of criticism and literary history to include those works with roots deep in the oral and musical patterns of Afro-American life" (42). Further, he concludes that "Jazz Literature demands a special form of criticism by inviting a synthesis of music and literature in a critical standard, a binding together of the two major language traditions [Afro-American and Anglo-American] into a self-conscious literary community, and a democratic one at that" (49).

But the reception by jazz critics of what I call jazz in fiction has been generally negative. Seldom do we find a really favorable review of a story with a strong jazz content. A good example of what I mean are these comments by Orrin Keepnews, a highly regarded record producer and jazz critic: "Usually, jazz novels are the work of terribly earnest young literary rebels, all full of Art and the Struggle of the Creative Artist and similar turgidity, and charitable folks can excuse them by attributing it all to their being young, or being friends of Jack Kerouac, or things like that" (34). On the whole, he characterizes these works as "pseudo-knowledgeable novels that falsify the jazz life in purple prose" (18). However, he is generally charitable in his comments about Dorothy Baker's *Young Man With a Horn*, Henry Steig's *Send Me Down*, and Harold Sinclair's *Music Out of Dixie*. But he questions, "And when is someone who has some knowledge and understanding of jazz—and therefore is qualified to relate properly the specifics of the jazz setting to the universalities of life—going to write a novel you can read without squirming?" (34)

Keepnews has some justifiable concerns, and he doesn't mince words. For example, he says that John Clellon Holmes's *The Horn* "is bad because Mr. Holmes doesn't know and thinks he does. Few things are worse than the hipness of the ignorant" (32). Of Garson Kanin's *Blow Up a Storm*, he says, "The problem is once again, as it so often is, that those who choose to write fiction about jazz don't really know the first thing about the music and those who live with and by it" (33).

But the problem of accuracy is always of concern for writers of fiction. Firsthand experience, however, doesn't always produce first-rate story-telling. Stephen Crane is proclaimed by many critics to have written a wonderfully accurate account in his *The Red Badge of Courage* of what Civil War soldiers and battles were like, though he never directly participated in the Civil War. In interrelations among the arts—in this case music and creative writing—the problem of accuracy and "truth" may be exceptionally formidable. Steven Scher says,

> Literary texts cannot transcend the confines of literary texture and become musical texture. Literature lacks the unique acoustic quality of music; only through ingenious linguistic means or special literary techniques can it imply, evoke, imitate, or otherwise indirectly approximate actual music and thus create what amounts at best to a verbal semblance of music. Firmly anchored in the literary realm, manifestations of music in literature promise to be most rewarding for literary study. (229)

Of course, Scher here seems to be most concerned with transmitting with text the actual sounds of music. In jazz fiction, though there is much more involved, often things are more simple than they might seem to be..

The first time I taught "Sonny's Blues" to a university class, I was not surprised to learn that the students had almost no knowledge whatsoever of these three all-important aspects of the story: the blues, Louis Armstrong, and Charlie Parker. I felt that if no attention were paid to the importance of these three elements in discussing the story, much would be lost that is very elementary but, at the same time, very essential. The same is true of Eudora Welty's classic "Powerhouse," which introduces a dynamic character inspired by the talented, vibrant, and uniquely original jazz pianist, Fats Waller, and which implies much about the life of an on-the-road jazz musician in the 1930s and 1940s. This is not to say that readings of these stories without knowledge of the jazz allusions are fruitless, but certainly Baldwin (especially) and Welty have been short-changed by readers who do not bring with them at least a cursory knowledge of jazz and blues which may be relatively straightforward, simple facts about jazz that writers do not need to have experienced firsthand, but which are very important in producing a work that has the ring of truth.

However, we must gather these simple facts with care and be aware of stereotyping. Shirley Anne Williams in "The Black Musician: The Black Hero as Light Bearer" emphasizes the importance of Black music as "the chief artifact created out of the Black experience" and notes that the music and musicians "are generally touched upon lightly and rarely explored as a theme deserving of individual and primary treatment," but rather "with a hedonistic, often raffish, sometimes shiftless, way of life which is in conflict with or depicted in contrast to conventional morality and respectability" (136). With references to Baldwin's "Sonny's Blues," *Another Country*, and *Blues for Mister Charlie*, she provides a more realistic account of the use of black music as metaphor and the black musician as one who deals in dreams and in love.

In the research community, a creditable amount has been done with reference to poetry, and in the area of fiction there has been a good start. This is indicated in this bibliography by the number of thought-provoking articles that focus on the music and the musicians, especially jazz icons such as Charlie Parker, Louis Armstrong, Billie Holiday, John Coltrane, and Lester Young. But the comments of Jones, Berry, and Williams strongly suggest the need for more study and critical examination of the interrelationship of jazz and both fiction and poetry. Hopefully, this bibliography will help to stimulate more research by providing a better idea of the works that have been touched by jazz and the blues and the kinds of critical discussions that have already been published.

Works Cited

Baldwin, James. "Sonny's Blues." *Going to Meet the Man*. New York: Dial Press, 1965. 103-141.

Berry, Jason. "Jazz Literature." *Southern Exposure* 6.3 (Fall 1978): 22-30.

Cortázar, Julio. "The Pursuers." *End of the Game and Other Stories*. Translated by Paul Blackburn. New York: Pantheon, 1967. 182-247.

Federman, Raymond. *Take It or Leave It: An Exaggerated second-hand tale to be read aloud either standing or sitting*. New York: Fiction Collective, 1976.

Grennard, Elliot. "Sparrow's Last Jump." *Harper's Magazine* May 1947: 419-426.

Holmes, John Clellon. *The Horn*. New York: Random House, 1958.

Jones, Gayl. "The Freeing of Traditional Forms: Jazz and Amiri Baraka's 'The Screamers.'" Chapter 10 in her *Liberating Voices: Oral Tradition in African American Literature*. Cambridge: Harvard UP, 1991. 111-122.

Keepnews, Orrin. *The View From Within: Jazz Writings 1948-1987*. New York: Oxford UP, 1988.

Kelley, William Melvin. *A Drop of Patience*. New York: Doubleday, 1965. Reprint Chatham, NJ: Chatham Booksellers, 1973.

Knight, Arthur, and Knight, Kit. *Interior Geographies: An Interview With John Clellon Holmes*. Warren, OH: the Literary Denim, 1981.

Newquist, Roy. *Conversations*. N.p.: Rand McNally, 1967.

Russell, Ross. *The Sound*. New York: E. P. Dutton, 1961.

Scher, Steven Paul. "Literature and Music." *Interrelations of Literature*. Ed. Jean-Pierre Barricelli and Joseph Gibaldi. New York: Modern Language Association of America, 1982. 225-250.

Scott, Tony. "Destination K. C." *The Jazz Word*. Ed. Dom Cerulli, Burt Korall, and Mort Nasatir. New York: Ballantine Books, Inc., 1960. 80-83.

Smith, Hugh L. Jr. *The Literary Manifestation of a Liberal Romanticism in American Jazz*. Diss. U New Mexico, 1955. Ann Arbor: UMI, 1973.

—. "Jazz in the American Novel." *English Journal* XLVII.8 (November 1958): 467-478.

Williams, John A. *Nightsong*. NY: Farrar, Straus and Cudahy, 1961.

Williams, Shirley Anne. "The Black Musician: The Black Hero as Light Bearer." Chapter Five in her *Give Birth to Brightness*. New York: Dial Press, 1972. 135-166.

ANTHOLOGIES

1. Albert, Richard N., ed. *From Blues to Bop: A Collection of Jazz Fiction.*
   Baton Rouge: Louisiana State UP, 1990.

   —. —. New York: Anchor Books/Doubleday, 1992.

   A collection of seventeen short stories and excerpts from three novels. See
   the entries noted for stories by these authors: Alston Anderson (103), James
   Baldwin (110), Donald Barthelme (116), Marshall Brickman (125), Beth
   Brown (126), Monty Culver (139), Leonard Feather (210), Shelby Foote
   (160), Elliott Grennard (169), Langston Hughes (43), John Clellon Holmes
   (174), Jack Kerouac (182), Willard Manus (201), Pamela Painter (225),
   J. F. Powers (229), Josef Škvorecký (247), and Eudora Welty (264).

2. Breton, Marcela, ed. *Hot and Cool: Jazz Short Stories.* New York: Plume,
   1990.

   A collection of nineteen short stories. See the entries noted for stories by
   these authors: Maya Angelou (104), James Baldwin (110), Toni Cade
   Bambara (113), Donald Barthelme (116), Julio Cortázar (137), Peter De
   Vries (144), Rudolph Fisher (159), Martin Gardner (164), Langston Hughes
   (177), LeRoi Jones (186), Willard Marsh (202), Ann Petry (225),
   J. F. Powers (229), Josef Škvorecký (247), C. W. Smith (251), Terry
   Southern (253), Eudora Welty (264), Al Young (268), and Richard Yates
   (267).

3. Cerulli, Dom, Burt Korall, and Mort Nasatir, eds. *The Jazz Word.* New
   York: Ballantine, 1960.

Has a fiction section with selections by James Baldwin (110), John Clellon Holmes (172), and Tony Scott (239).

4. Condon, Eddie and Richard Gehman, eds. *Eddie Condon's Treasury of Jazz.* New York: Dial, 1956.

Not primarily an anthology of jazz fiction, but it includes a selection of short stories. See the entries for these authors: Charles Beaumont (117), Osborn Duke (146), Shelby Foote (160), James Jones (185), Gerald Kersh (190), and Robert Sylvester (260).

5. Harvey, Charles, ed. *Jazz Parody (Anthology of Jazz Fiction).* London: Spearman Publishers Ltd., 1948.

A collection of thirteen short stories. See the entries for these authors: Alex Austin (106), David Boyce (122), Pat Brand (123), Ward Dabinett (141), Archie Douglas (145), Robert Evans (151, 152), Charles Fox (161), Phil Garceau (163), Albert J. McCarthy (205), Frederic Ramsey, Jr. (231), and Peter Shirley (242, 243).

6. Lange, Art, and Nathaniel Mackey, ed. *Moment's Notice: Jazz in Poetry and Prose.* Minneapolis: Coffee House Press, 1993.

Along with a large and varied selection of poetry, the classic jazz stories of James Baldwin (110), Eudora Welty (264), J. F. Powers (229), and Henry Dumas (148) are included. There are also excerpts of longer works by Evan Hunter, Julio Cortázar, Michael Ondaatje, Jack Kerouac, and John Clellon Holmes.

7. Parker, Chris, ed. *B Flat, Bebop, Scat.* London: Quartet, 1986.

Contains never-before-published short stories, along with a selection of poems. Please see the entries for these authors: Patrick Biggie (149), Campbell Burnap (130), Elaine Cohen (134), Clive Davis (142), Digby Fairweather (153), Julio Finn (158), Kitty Grime (170), William J. Moody (219), Ed Neiderhiser (222), and Robert Tilley (261).

NOVELS

8. Adams, Alice. *Listening to Billie*. New York: Knopf, 1978.

   —. —. New York: Viking Penguin, 1984.

   —. —. New York: Ballantine Books, 1991

   Story of poet Eliza Hamilton, intertwined with the memory of having heard Billie Holiday one night in the 1950s. Eliza keeps coming back to thoughts of Billie as she deals with the problems and tragedies of her own life.

9. Baker, Dorothy. *Young Man With a Horn*. New York: Houghton Mifflin, 1938.

   —. —. New York: Editions for the Armed Services, 1938.

   —. —. New York: Press of the Readers Club, 1943.

   —. — New York: Sun Dial Press, 1944.

   —. —. New York: New American Library (A Signet Book), 1945, 1953.

   —. —. New York: World Publishing Co. (Tower Books Ed.), 1946.

   Story of Rick Martin, trumpet player, based on the legendary Bix Beiderbecke. Emphasized is the conflict many jazz musicians experience between being able to improvise and being held down as a chart player in the big bands. Rick is another jazz hero bent on self-destruction and anticipates the self-destructive life of another jazz legend, Charlie Parker.

10. Baldwin, James. *Another Country*. New York: Dial, 1962.

—. —. New York: Dell, 1985.

—. —. New York: Vintage, 1993.

This novel has minor jazz significance. The central character, Rufus, is a jazz musician.

11. Barnes, Harper. *Blue Monday*. St. Louis: Patrice Press, 1991.

Novice Kansas City *Journal-Post* reporter and jazz lover Michael Holt suspects foul play in the death of Bennie Moten during a tonsillectomy. The setting is April 1935 in Kansas City. Michael feels that there might be a drug connection because of the growing hard drug traffic in K.C. at that time. As he investigates, the reader is given a detailed review of the news of the day, along with numerous jazz scenes involving references to Count Basie, Lester Young, Hershel Evans, Jimmy Rushing, Earl Hines, and others who played in the city at that time. Barnes also, in several scenes, brings in a young alto sax player named Charles and describes his attempts to sit in and solo during various jam sessions. In an Afterword, Barnes acknowledges this obvious reference to Charlie Parker.

12. Bontemps, Arna. *Lonesome Boy*. Boston: Houghton Mifflin, 1955.

A very short juvenile "novel" (28 pages) about a young black boy who wants to play trumpet. Illustrated by Feliks Topolski.

13. Borneman, Ernest. *Tremolo*. New York: Harper, 1948.

—. —. London: Jarrolds, 1948.

—. —. London: Four Square Books, 1960.

A mystery novel of sorts in which Mike Sommerville attempts to find out the cause of strange, almost seemingly supernatural, occurrences in his family's life. Jazz enters into the novel by way of Mike's being a former jazz clarinetist who now runs a musical instrument manufacturing business, but who still has jazz friends and sits in with those who are active in the profession. There are many references to Chicago style jazz greats, with special reference to clarinetist Leon Rappolo. It is also interesting to note that the storyteller says, "If you play jazz, you've got to drink" (81).

14. Bourjaily, Vance. *The Great Fake Book*. New York: Weidenfeld & Nicolson, 1987.

When Charles Mizzourin was only an infant, his father Mike died. Thirty years later, Charles searches his father's past, trying to find out as much as he can. He discovers parts of an autobiography, "The Great Fake Book," Mike had written and learns that Mike had been obsessed with jazz after getting out of the service when World War II ended. The novel's jazz content resides in Mike's memoirs. The rest of the story involves Charles's political career in Washington as aide to an Iowa congressman who runs for re-election against Charles's uncle.

15. Braly, Malcolm. *Shake Him Till He Rattles*. New York: Fawcett, 1963.

—. —. New York: Pocket Books, 1976.

A detective novel with a somewhat minor jazz significance, but it has some great descriptive passages depicting a jam session and other jazz performances. The novel focuses on San Francisco narcotics policeman Lieut. Carver's obsession with catching jazz saxophonist Lee Cabiness on a narcotics charge. Has a jazz club called "Bird's Nest."

16. Cartiér, Xam Wilson. *Be-Bop, Re-Bop*. New York: Available-Ballantine, 1987.

The black, female narrator tells of her life as a child and young woman growing up in St. Louis and on her own as a single mother in San Francisco. Jazz enters into this polemical story mostly in relation to her father, Double, who loved jazz and taught his daughter about it. There are many references to famous artists such as Charlie Parker, John Coltrane, Benny Goodman, Fletcher Henderson, Ethel Waters, and Billie Holiday. Comments are made about jazz and the blues being the music of blacks and that bebop was a revolt against whites stealing the music. The story is told in a style that employs much rhyme and alliteration.

17. —. —.. *Muse-Echo Blues*. New York: Harmony, 1991.

The central character is Kat, who narrates the story from 1990 San Francisco and moves back and forth in time, becoming Kitty in Kansas City in 1945 and Lena in 1933. She is a composer who can't become inspired and fantasizes about the past: "the past was the place to go when I was mad, sad, or too glad to stand it; past eras were full of more life than the now where I sustain my self-inflicted identity. . . . I'm a woman in search of my own need to be" (177). Along the way there are references to a host of jazz musicians: Charlie Parker, Louis Armstrong, Duke Ellington, Billie Holiday, Miles Davis, Billy Eckstine, Jay McShann, Jimmie Lunceford, Chick Webb, Fletcher Henderson, Illinois Jacquet, Sonny Stitt, Count Basie, and Lester Young. The style of writing is much the same as in Cartier's *Be-Bop, Re-Bop*.

18. Catling, Patrick Bruce. *Jazz Jazz Jazz*. New York: St. Martin's, 1981.

Traces the history of jazz, from Storyville down to the 1970s through the career of white jazz pianist Al Dexter who through the years becomes involved in all the various jazz styles, from Armstrong through Parker and bebop. Social concerns, such as drugs, prostitution, and racism are all given emphasis.

19. Charters, Samuel. *Jelly Roll Morton's Last Night at the Jungle Inn: An Imaginary Memoir by Samuel Charters*. New York: Marion Boyars, 1984.

Charters acknowledges his indebtedness to a number of sources, especially Alan Lomax, in his telling of this story. He mixes fact and fiction as he has Jelly Roll tell his own story to a patron at his Jungle Inn in Washington, D. C., on an evening in 1940. Morton is portrayed as a man with a very large ego who claims to have invented jazz and to have been superior to all other jazzmen when it came to playing the piano, composing, and arranging. He tells of his travels from New Orleans in the early 1900s throughout the United States, with emphasis on Los Angeles, Chicago, and New York.

20. Collier, James Lincoln. *The Jazz Kid*. New York: Henry Holt, 1994.

A piece of juvenile fiction set in 1920s Chicago. Paulie Horvath, in his early teens, is captivated by jazz and is determined to make it his life's career, over the objections of his plumber father and his mother. Failing in school, he runs away and lives with his cornet mentor. In the process of finding himself, Paulie runs into Chicago gangsters and jazz legends such as Louis Armstrong, King Oliver, and Bix Beiderbecke.

21. Conroy, Frank. *Body & Soul*. New York: Houghton Mifflin, 1993.

A long (450 pages) novel that has as its central character a piano prodigy, Claude Rawlings. His career is traced from his early youth in New York after World War II to his careeer as a concert pianist. Conroy shows his knowledge of music through his detailed descriptions of Claude's early studies and practices. Jazz enters into the story through his also being attracted to jazz and the final revelation that his father was, and is, a jazz pianist.

22. Curran, Dale. *Dupree Blues*. New York: Knopf, 1948.

Has a pretty typical plot for a "jazz" novel of this time. The main characters play in a dance band and have dreams of having a real jazz band in Memphis. Dupree is a trombonist who is ruined by gambling. He kills a jeweler arguing about payment for a ring he gives to Betty, the band's vocalist, and is himself shot. Overall, the novel presents a credible picture of the jazzman's life.

23. —. *Piano in the Band.* New York: Reynal, 1940.

Traces the career of pianist George Baker as he strives to find himself within the confines of a popular swing band led by Jeff Walters, a tyrannical band leader who is afraid to let his players try new things. Not until George has contact with black jazz pianist Rink Stevens does he begin to have any faith in his own worth. The novel ends with Rink and George having plans to start a racially mixed jazz band in New York.

24. Cuthbert, Clifton. *The Robbed Heart.* New York: Fischer, 1945.

A white jazz critic falls in love with a light-skinned black woman. Jazz is simply a backdrop for relating their problems.

25. Duke, Osborn. *Sideman.* New York: Criterion, 1956.

Emphasizes the life of on-the-road big band musicians, in this case through central character Bernie Bell, a trombonist whose real goal in life is to compose. He falls in love with Claire Lyons, a dancer, and devotes his time to composing a dance suite for her. Through the novel there are references to Charlie Parker, Louis Armstrong, Stan Kenton, and others, along with jam session scenes and the new bebop style.

26. Dyer, Geoff. *But Beautiful.* London: Jonathan Cape, 1991.

Difficult to classify as strictly either fiction or non-fiction. Dyer presents portraits of Lester Young, Thelonious Monk, Bud Powell, Ben Webster, Charlie Mingus, Chet Baker, and Art Pepper. In his preface, he refers to his presentation as "imaginative criticism" and fiction. He does his "own versions" on commonly known information, "stating the identifying facts more or less briefly and then improvising around them, departing from them completely in some cases" (ix). Some episodes, he says, have "wholly invented scenes [that] can be seen as original composition" (x).

27. Ewing, Annemarie. *Little Gate.* New York: Rinehart, 1947.

A swing era, big-band setting novel that traces the career of Joe Geddes from Iowa to Chicago and to New York.

28. Flender, Harold. *Paris Blues*. New York: Ballantine, 1957.

    —. —. London: Hamilton, 1961.

    Story of expatriate saxophonist Eddie Cook and his love affair with American teacher/tourist Connie Mitchell. Gives a dim, negative view of jazz in the United States: "stinking union," "grubby managers," "gangsters and vultures who want their boys to be coke-heads or hop-heads or mainliners. . . ."

29. Gant, Roland. *World in a Jug*. London: Jonathan Cape, 1959.

    —. —. New York: Vanguard, 1961.

    Larry Alden, white jazz musician, gives a first-person account (via a tape-recording) of his life from 1920s New Orleans to his life in Europe. Has strong jazz references, both to musicians and to the music.

30. Gilbert, Edwin. *The Hot and the Cool*. New York: Doubleday, 1953.

    —. —. N.p. : Popular Library, 1954.

    Kip Nelson, jazz pianist who is "less than a man" after an auto accident, seeks to break with the old style jazz that he loves and "say something his own way with jazz . . ."

31. Green, Benny. *Fifty-Eight Minutes to London*. London: MacGibbon & Kee, 1969.

    Set in the early 1950s in Brighton, England, this is the story of young dance band musicians struggling to make it in jazz. An insightful picture of the dance hall scene.

32. Guralnick, Peter. *Nighthawk Blues*. New York: Seaview, 1980.

    —. —. New York: Thunder's Mouth Press, 1988.

    Aging blues legend Nighthawk Jefferson heads home from New York City to his home in Yola, Mississippi after an auto accident. He is followed by his agent, Jerry, who reflects on how he first found Jefferson and represented him nationwide. Will be of great interest to blues aficionados of the Delta bluesmen of the 1920s-1940s.

33. Gwinn, William. *Jazz Bum*. New York: Lion, 1954.

A paperback original that stresses the sensational aspects of "the jazz life." The main character, Vic Ravenna, is dedicated to jazz, but his life is made difficult by alcohol and by his obsessive love for Zora, a woman who wanted fame and money at any cost.

34. Hardwick, Elizabeth. *Sleepless Nights.* New York: Random House, 1979.

—. —. New York: Vintage, 1990.

Chapter 3 has important references to Billie Holiday in the 1940s. New York's Hotel Schuyler on W. 45th Street is where the female narrator lives with a male homosexual. The chapter conveys a nihilistic impression of Billie's life: "Is this all there is? Her work took on, gradually, a destructive cast, as it so often does with the greatly gifted who are doomed to repeat endlessly their own heights of inspiration."

35. Hentoff, Nat. *Jazz Country.* New York: Harper, 1965; 1976.

—. —. New York: Dell, A Mayflower Book, 1967, 1986.

A piece of juvenile fiction about a young boy, Tom Curtis, who aspires to be a jazz trumpeter because of the influence of black jazz musicians, especially Moses Godfrey, a Thelonious Monk inspired character, who becomes the young narrator's mentor. Tom, as he approaches high school graduation, faces the decision of whether to go on to college or rather try to get into jazz immediately. The novel has strong civil rights statements and is as much polemical as it is jazz centered.

36. Herzhaft, Gerard. *Long Blues in A Minor.* Trans. John DuVal. Fayetteville: U Arkansas P, 1988.

The French narrator, after World War II, becomes inspired, through listening to blues records given to him by an American army sergeant, to find legendary bluesman Big Johnny White, which he does. Along the way, he learns that the blues express suffering. The story has a basic initiation theme.

37. Hesse, Herman. *Steppenwolf.* Cutchogue, New York: Buccaneer Books, 1976.

—. —. New York: Bantam, 1983.

—. —. New York: Owl Books, 1990.

Published in 1927, *Steppenwolf* is the story of Harry Haller's intellectual self-examination with reference to spirit vs. flesh (man vs. wolf). One of the characters in the story is Pablo, a jazz saxophonist who is presented as a stereotype in that his lifestyle is portrayed as hedonistic. Pablo urges Harry to leave his personality behind and find the world in his soul, which involves giving into his instincts and impulses. Harry initially refers to jazz lovers as "idlers and pleasure seekers" (136). Pablo prefers to simply play music rather than talk about it. He says, "Music does not depend on being right, on having good taste and education and all that" (149).

38. Hewat, Alan V. *Lady's Time*. New York: Harper and Row, 1985.

Set in the blues and jazz milieu of turn-of-the-century New Orleans. The central character is Alice Beaudette, who plays ragtime piano. She runs off to Vermont and plays piano in a resort to escape her father. Her life is affected by voodoo and jazz.

39. Hill, Richard. *Riding Solo with the Golden Horde*. Athens, GA: U Georgia P, 1994.

High school senior Vic Messenger reads *Down Beat*, plays sax, and pursues what he perceives to be the life of a jazz musician—gigging, drinking, sampling drugs, and pursuing women. The author has a special fondness for player Gene Quill, a less well-known 1950s jazz player who succumbed to drugs and died at age 61. The story is classified as "Teenagers—Fiction."

40.. Holmes, John Clellon. *Go!* New York: Scribner's, 1952.

—. —. New York: Ace, 1958.

—. —. as *The Beat Boys*. London: Harborough, 1959.

—. —. Mamaroneck, New York: Paul Appel, 1977

.—. —. New York: Thunder's Mouth Press, 1988.

Not a "jazz novel," this first Beat Generation novel, much like Kerouac's *On the Road*, reveals the Beats' attraction to jazz in its many references to the music and musicians.

41. —. *The Horn*. New York: Random House, 1958.

—. —. Greenwich, Connecticut: Fawcett (A Crest Reprint), 1959.

—.—. London: Andre Deutsch, 1959.

—.—. Berkeley, California: Creative Arts, 1980.

—.—. New York: Thunder's Mouth Press, 1988.

A very strongly jazz-oriented Beat Generation novel with a central character; Edgar "The Horn" Pool, inspired by both Lester Young and Charlie
Parker. It deals with the decline of Edgar and his attempts to recapture his
former glory. Other characters reflect Dizzy Gillespie, Billie Holiday, and
Thelonious Monk. It is also a novel that relates its jazz artists to nineteenth
century literary artists Melville, Poe, Hawthorne, Whitman, and Dickinson.
Given a negative review by Orrin Keepnews in 1958 in *The Jazz Review*, the
novel in its most recent Thunder's Mouth edition was, in its introduction,
praised by jazz musician Archie Shepp.

42. Houston, James D. *Gig*. New York: Dial, 1969.

—. —. Berkeley, California: Creative Arts, 1989.

An evening at a piano bar with pianist Roy Ambrose and a variety of
patrons. Emphasizes that Roy would rather not be catering to the wishes of
an often drunken and raucous clientele. Many of the tunes Roy plays are
standards by the likes of Cole Porter, Rodgers and Hart, and Hoagy
Carmichael.

43. Hughes, Langston. *Not Without Laughter*. New York: Knopf, 1930.

—. —. New York: Collier Books, 1969.

Chapter 8, "Dance," depicts jazz as an important part of black culture, and
dancing as an important means of emotional release. Hughes emphasizes
the blues—"the plain old familiar, heart-breaking and extravagant, my-
baby's-gone-from-me blues"—and the individuality shown by both dancers
and musicians.

44. Hunter, Evan. *Second Ending*. New York: Simon and Schuster, 1956.

—. —. as *Quartet in "H."* New York: Pocket Books, 1957.

—. —. New York: Avon Books, 1976.

Andy Silvera, young jazz trumpeter, has a drug problem and prevails upon
his good friend, college student Bud Donato, to help him. A tragic end for
Silvera has a positive effect on Donato's character. The jazz background in
this story rings true.

45. —. *Streets of Gold*. New York: Harper & Row, 1974.

—. —. New York: Ballantine, 1975.

—. —. New York: Stein and Day, 1985.

Fifty-second Street in New York is the "street of gold" in this novel about Ignazio ("Iggie") Palermo (later, Dwight Jamison), a blind son of Italian immigrants who worships Art Tatum and is caught up in the 1940s bebop revolution as he strives to become a great jazz pianist. The story has many references to jazz musicians, such as Dizzy Gillespie, Oscar Peterson, Erroll Garner, Marian McPartland, and George Shearing, as well as some very descriptive passages of jazz performances. In a note at the end of the novel, Hunter thanks John Mehegan "—the jazz pianist, teacher, and writer—for sharing . . . his own love for the piano, and his vast understanding of this unique art form."

46. Hunter, Kristin. *God Bless the Child*. New York: Scribner's, 1964.

—. —. Washington, D. C.: Howard UP, 1987.

Though the heroine of this novel is not a jazz singer and this is not a jazz novel, the tragic life of the heroine, Rosie, reflects the hard, troubled life of Billie Holiday.

47. Jeffers, H. Paul. *Rubout at the Onyx*. New Haven and New York: Ticknor and Fields, 1981.

Set in the mid-1930s in New York, this detective mystery follows private detective Harry McNeil's efforts to solve a murder and find $3 million of stolen diamonds. A jazz lover, Harry's office is above the famed Onyx Club on 52nd Street. Though not heavily jazz oriented, there are direct encounters with Art Tatum, George Gershwin, and Paul Whiteman, among others.

48. Jones, Gayl. *Corregidora*. New York: Random House, 1975.

—. —. Boston: Beacon Press, 1986.

The central character, Ursa Corregidora, is a blues singer, but the novel is not strongly jazz/blues oriented. It is primarily a deep character study of male/female relationships that are often brutal.

49. Kanin, Garson. *Blow Up a Storm*. New York: Random House, 1959.

—. —. London: Heinemann, 1960.

—. —. London: Hamilton, 1961.

The playwright/saxophonist narrator recalls what happened back in the 1930s to Woody Woodruff and his mixed-race jazz combo. The story has a strong jazz element, with many references to real jazz musicians and styles, but it tends to dwell too much on the excessive use of drugs and booze.

50. —. *The Rat Race.* New York: Pocket Books, Inc., 1960. (Originally *The Rat Race: A Play in Three Acts,* published in 1950.)

A simple story of a young, naive jazz saxophonist from Milwaukee, Pete Hammer, who travels to New York to make his fortune but whose romantic notions are destroyed by reality. More a love story of a young man and woman seeking to overcome adversity in the big city, but Pete's attraction to Lee Konitz and Gerry Mulligan is evident.

51. Kelley, William Melvin. *A Drop of Patience.* New York: Doubleday, 1965.

—. —. Chatham, New Jersey: Chatham Booksellers, 1973.

Blind-from-birth jazz alto-saxophonist Ludlow Washington becomes the leader of a jazz combo. Interestingly, his instrument is never specifically named, but only alluded to. He therefore seems to represent all artists who suffer in their efforts to achieve "truth."

52. Kerouac, Jack. *On the Road.* New York: Viking, 1957.

—. —. London: Deutsch, 1958.

—. —. London: Pan, 1961.

—. —. New York: Viking Penguin, 1976.

53. —. *The Subterraneans.* New York: Grove, 1958.

—. —. London: Deutsch, 1960.

—. —. New York: Grove/Atlantic, 1989.

Neither *On the Road* nor *The Subterraneans* is a "jazz novel," but both, especially *On the Road*, have the spontaneity of jazz and many jazz passages that mention well-known jazz musicians, from Charlie Parker to Brew Moore, and that convey the excitement of jazz performances. Kerouac's

"Jazz of the Beat Generation"(see Item 182) eventually became a part of *On the Road*, though in somewhat altered form.

54. Lea, George. *Somewhere There's Music*. Philadelphia: Lippincott, 1958.

Another novel with a self-destructive jazz musician, saxophonist Mike Logan, home from the war in Korea and with no real goal in life. There is strong emphasis on what some would call the "beat" life style, with heavy use of drink and drugs.

55. Lively, Adam. *Blue Fruit*. New York: Simon and Schuster, 1987.

John Field, an eighteenth-century "errant time traveler" leaves a whaler and finds himself in twentieth-century New York. Given lodging by an African-American family, this classically trained violinist is introduced to jazz and becomes a member of a group. A brief exposure to work in corporate America drives him back to jazz and his African-American friends.

56. Malone, R. Pingank. *Sound Your "A": The Story of Trumpeter Tom Stewart in Full-Length Form*. *Metronome* September 1942:16-17, 22; October 1942: 14-15, 22; November 1942: 14-15, 20-21; December 1942: 14-15, 27, 30; February 1943: 16-17, 24.

A serial form novel that is divided into twenty-five chapters and was published in five issues of the magazine. It is the story of a group of struggling swing musicians who aspire to play jazz but are restricted by having to play in dance bands, such as the "tickety-tockety" bands that were prevalent in the 1940s. There are many references to popular bands of that time, such as Charlie Barnet and Woody Herman. The story seemed to be very popular with *Metronome* readers, as is indicated by the ire of some readers who complained that the January 1943 issue failed to include the next installment of the serial.

57. Martucci, Ida. *Jive Jungle*. New York: Vantage, 1956.

Basically, a simple love story with a jazz background. There are many references to real jazz musicians, like Howard McGhee, Machito, Stan Getz, and Charlie Parker.

58. McCluskey, John. *Look What They Done to My Song*. New York: Random House, 1974.

Mack, a blues-inspired saxophonist, sees music as a way of bringing people together. In the end he is a preacher who plays blues in the church..

59. McKay, Claude. *Home to Harlem*. New York: Harper & Brothers, 1928.

—. —. New York: Pocket Cardinal, 1965.

—. —. Boston: Northeastern UP, 1987.

Chapter IV, "Congo Rose," pp. 28-40, presents a picture of Harlem cabaret life in the 1920s and emphasizes blues as an inherent part of black culture and an expression of the realities of black urban life.

60. Millen, Gilmore. *Sweet Man*. London: Cassell, 1930.

—. —.New York: Viking, 1930.

Not a jazz novel, though there are some references to the blues and some vivid pictures of Beale Street in Memphis. The story traces the career of John Henry from the late 1800s through World War I. There is a graphic description of mob justice—the burning of an innocent black man.

61. Morrison, Toni. *Jazz*. New York: Alfred A. Knopf, 1992.

The story of Violet and Joe Trace, his affair with young Dorcas Manfred, and Joe's subsequent killing of Dorcas and Violet's cutting of Dorcas's face at the funeral, told from various points of view, which are like variations on a theme in a jazz piece. There are also references to jazz, blues, and dancing.

62. Murray, Albert. *Train Whistle Guitar*. New York: McGraw-Hill, 1974.

—. —. Boston: Northeastern UP, 1989.

The novel-length version of Murray's 1953 short story. Scooter, the narrator, reminisces about his early life with his friend Little Buddy in Gasoline Point, Alabama in the 1930s. He is very much influenced by itinerant guitarist Luzana Cholly, who early in the novel preaches the importance of education. The story has a number of jazz and blues references, especially to piano players Stagolee Dupas and Claiborne Williams, which serve to indicate the importance of music in the lives of many of the people in the South at that time.

63. Neil, Al. *Changes*. Toronto: Coach House Press, 1976.

—. —. London, Ontario: Nightwood Editions, 1989.

In this autobiographical novel, Al Neil assumes the identity of Seamus Finn, jazz pianist, who says that he is writing this for himself. His self-reflections emphasize his drug addiction and his, at times, surrealistic style reminds one of Williams Burroughs's *Naked Lunch*. The locale is Vancouver, British Columbia. Chapter 9 has comments on conformity among some jazz musicians and their need to break new ground. Chapter 14 discusses the relationship of players to their audiences and the effect of drugs on playing. In Chapter 23, Seamus philosophizes on jazz as art and jazz as musical language.

64. Oliphant, Robert. *A Trumpet For Jackie*. Englewood Cliffs, New Jersey: Prentice-Hall, 1983.

The story of Jackie Hayes, who goes from jazz trumpet player to bandleader to radio personality to producer. However, the success Jackie achieves in these areas does not allow him to let go of his love for jazz and his desire to play the trumpet. He listens to bands to see if "they play any real jazz." He has a big decision to make when an opportunity arises to sell his production company and practice for a solo jazz performance. To Jackie, jazz music was the art of tapping the listener's memory through a familiar melody stated and then improvised upon.

65. Ondaatje, Michael. *Coming Through Slaughter*. Toronto: House of Anansi Press, 1976.

—. —. New York: W. W. Norton, 1976.

—. —. London: M. Boyars, 1979.

—. —. New Press Canadian Classics series. Toronto: General, 1982.

—. —. New York: Viking Penguin, 1984.

Based on the life of jazz cornetist Buddy Bolden, this story concentrates not on his music but on his obsession with women and his paranoia. Ondaatje presents the flavor of turn-of-the-century Storyville.

66. Phillips, Jane. *Mojo Hand*. New York: Trident, 1969.

—. —. Berkeley: City Miner's Books, 1985.

Has a character, bluesman Blacksnake Brown, who grew out of Phillips's close observations of Sam "Lightnin'" Hopkins. The central character is mulatto Eunice Prideaux, who is searching for her identity.

67. Plater, Alan. *Misterioso*. London: Methuen, 1987.

Rachael searches for the father she never knew—a man mysteriously related to Thelonious Monk's tune "Misterioso." This British story has a few strong jazz musician characters and many references to jazz greats and jazz tunes.

68. Reed, Harlan. *The Swing Music Murder*. New York: Dutton, 1938.

A hard-boiled detective story with a Seattle setting and a swing music background.

69. Richards-Slaughter, Shannon. *The Blossoms of Jazz: A Novel of Black Female Jazz Musicians in the 1930s*. Diss. U Michigan, 1990.

A novel written as a Ph.D. dissertation. Richards-Slaughter says in the abstract that "Although the novel is an imaginative attempt at re-creating some of the forgotten world of African-American musicianship and African-American culture as it existed in the 1930s, the novel also alludes to and discusses real musicians, conditions, events, and places that were part of that world and that culture."

70. Rundell, Wyatt. *Jazz Band*. New York: Greenburg, 1935.

A soap-opera-style love story set in Kansas City, Missouri. The central character is a dance band musician, but the novel as a whole is not very jazz flavored.

71. Russell, Ross. *The Sound*. New York: Dutton, 1961.

A very strong jazz novel with a Charlie Parker inspired central character, trumpet player Red Travers. Russell emphasizes Travers's musical genius but gives much more space to the character's self-destruction. Russell is the author of the Charlie Parker biography, *Bird Lives*, and the producer of the Parker's Dial recording sessions, including the famous "Lover Man" session. His personal experiences with Parker may have prompted Russell to devote much of the book to Travers's excesses.

72. Shurman, Ida. *Death Beats the Band*. New York: Phoenix, 1943.

Band leader Andy Parker is shot dead while singing during an engagement at the Log House. Snowed in by a blizzard, the guests and orchestra investigate his murder, led by bass player Jack Coler. The novel is very slight in its jazz content.

73. Sill, Harold. *Misbehavin' with Fats*. Illus. Mike Eagle. Reading, Mass.: Addison-Wesley, 1978.

A juvenile fantasy in which young Toby Bradley, after listening to some of his father's old Fats Waller's records, takes his dog for a walk and is confronted by Fats down by the riverside. He is spirited away by Fats to an on-the-road one-night stand, a day in the Harlem of Fats's childhood, a recording session, and a rent party. Along with getting to know Fats and members of his band (Gene Sedric, Herman Autrey, Al Casey), Toby also meets Eddie Condon, James P. Johnson, and Luckey Roberts.

74. Simmons, Herbert. *Man Walking on Eggshells*. Boston: Houghton Mifflin, 1962.

—. —. London: Methuen, 1962.

—. —. London: Jazz Book Club, 1964.

The central character is jazz trumpeter Raymond "Splib" Douglas, overindulgent but symbolic of hope for the black man. Splib is reminiscent of Miles Davis up to a point. The novel is divided into three parts, each titled with a tune related to Miles: "Walking," "So What?" and "'Round Midnight."

75. Simon, George T. *Don Watson Starts His Band*. New York: Dodd, Mead, 1941.

A juvenile novel about a young band leader crossing over from amateur to professional. The big band profession of the 1930s is highlighted. The forward is written by Benny Goodman.

76. Sinclair, Harold. *Music Out of Dixie*. New York: Rinehart, 1952.

—. —. New York: Perma Books, 1953.

Story of Dade Tarrant from age seven in 1905 through his years as a piano player in Storyville, on the road with a traveling minstrel show, and as a band leader in clubs and on a riverboat. There are many references to jazz greats like Johnny Dodds, Jelly Roll Morton, and Freddy Keppard.

77. Škvorecký, Josef. *The Cowards*. Trans. Jeanne Nemcova. New York: Grove, 1970.

—. —. London: Gollancz, 1970.

—. —. Toronto: Penguin Canada, 1980.

—. —. New York: Ecco Press, 1980.

A post-war story of Germans moving out of Czechoslovakia and Russians moving in. The central character is horn player Danny Smiricky, who loves jazz and plays in a small jazz band with his friends.

78. —. *The Swell Season*. Trans Paul Wilson. New York: Ecco Press, 1986.

To be read with *The Cowards* and "The Bass Saxophone" since they make up a trilogy centering on the life of Danny Smiricky. Here Danny is about seventeen and is living in Nazi occupied Czechoslovakia, where jazz is forbidden.

79. Smith, Julie. *Jazz Funeral*. New York: Fawcett Columbine, 1993.

—. —. New York: Ballantine/Ivy Books, 1994.

New Orleans homicide detective Skip Langdon investigates the murder of Hamson Brocato, producer of the annual Jazz and Heritage Festival. Despite the jazz festival setting, there is not a great deal here to demand the interest of jazz and blues enthusiasts.

80. Spicer, Bart. *Blues For the Prince*. New York: Dodd, Mead, 1950.

—. —. Harpenden, Herts, U.K.: No Exit Press, 1989.

Hard-boiled private investigator Carney Wilde investigates the death of Harold Morton Prince, renowned jazz/blues pianist and composer, while at the same time trying to prove that "The Prince" had not plagiarized his most famous songs. The story has some good jazz interludes (see "All-Prince Night" at Manny Brenner's HOT BOX on pages 180-193 of the No Exit Press edition). Spicer seems to understand hot jazz very well.

81. Steig, Henry. *Send Me Down*. New York: Knopf, 1941.

Highly romanticized, this novel touches on the life of big-band musicians in the 1930s and talks about the problems of marijuana, crooked agents, the difficulty of blacks getting into white bands, and interracial love. The two central characters are Frank, pianist who follows the commercial big-band route, and Pete, clarinetist who is materially less successful because he dedicates himself to small combo jazz.

82. Sylvester, Robert. *Rough Sketch*. New York: Dial, 1948.

This is a multi-faceted work. One section, Part 2, "Pops Jarman," is jazz oriented. It consists of Walter Homer Jarman's reminiscenses of Tony Fenner (agent) for a profile being done by Carl Myerly for *Current Magazine*. The section revolves around Frankie Watts, cornet player. The rest of the story is not jazz oriented.

83. Tate, Sylvia. *Never By Chance*. New York: Harper, 1947.

Basically a mystery/suspense novel that has a swing music background.

84. Tormé, Mel. *Wynner*. New York: Stein and Day, 1978.

—. —. London: Futura, 1980.

Mel Tormé uses his life experiences as a big band and jazz singer to chronicle the life of Marty Wynner, big band vocalist, with emphasis on the 1930s and 1940s. Much space is devoted to references to big name musicians like Benny Goodman and Billie Holliday [sic]. Chapter 24 has Marty singing with Lady Day.

85. Wain, John. *Strike the Father Dead*. London: Macmillan, 1962.

—. —. New York: St. Martins, 1962.

Jeremy Coleman pursues a career as a jazz pianist, much to the displeasure of his father Alfred, a professor of Greek. As he practices his art in London, he becomes friends with Percy, a black American. The setting is World War II. It has very good jazz description.

86. Weik, Mary Hays. *The Jazz Man*. Il. Ann Grifalconi. New York: Atheneum, 1966.

—. —. New York: Aladdin, 1993.

A story for elementary school, grades 4 and 5. About a nine-year-old black boy, Zeke, who because of a limp has an inferiority complex. He is inspired by a jazz pianist who moves into the neighborhood, but he is then abandoned by his parents. The jazz man also then leaves.

87. Westin, Jeane. *Swing Sisters*. New York: Scribner, 1991.

—. —. New York: Pinnacle, 1994.

Set in the late 1930s and early 1940s, this 500+ page novel chronicles the trials and tribulations of an all-girl swing band. The main character, a vocalist named Lovey, suffers a past that includes a broken marriage and the death of her three-year-old son in a fire. She fights alcohol and her passion for two men. The novel describes the tragic lives of the musicians when alcohol and drugs consume their lives. There are references throughout to jazz greats.

88. Whitmore, Stanford. *Solo*. New York: Harcourt, Brace, 1955.

—. —. London: Gollancz, 1956.

—. —. London: Transworld, 1958.

Enigmatic jazz pianist Virgil Jones is the epitome of individuality. He refuses to cater to others, especially jazz critics and promoters. He claims, "I AM THE LAST INDIVIDUAL IN THE WORLD" and almost seems to resent any form of human communication. He would be just as happy to play only by and for himself.

89. Williams, John A. *Night Song*. New York: Farrar, Straus, and Cudahy, 1961.

—. —. New York: Dell, 1963.

—. —. New York: Pocket Books, 1970.

The story of Charlie Parker-inspired Richie "Eagle" Stokes, an innovative bop saxophonist whose downfall is overindulgence. When he dies, he becomes a legend—the rebel who refuses to wear the Sambo smile. The novel emphasizes, through the white character, David Hillary, the alienation of blacks and whites and is probably most interested in talking about problems of racism.

90. Willis, George. *Little Boy Blues*. New York: Dutton, 1948.

Trumpeter Low Carey begins his career in Kansas City dives, but aspires to have his own band. He meets a woman who has the money to finance him.

91. —. *Tangleweed*. Garden City, New York: Doubleday, 1943.

A depressing view of a swing band drummer's life on-the-road and his aspirations to compose.

92. Young, Al. *Snakes*. New York: Holt, Rinehart and Winston, 1970.

—. —. London: Sidgwick & Jackson, 1971.

—. —. New York: Dell Laurel, 1972.

Not heavily jazz-oriented. The central character, M. C., plays guitar and has a small band. His life is fulfilled by the blues, which are noted to be an important form of release from sorrow. The story has many references to jazz greats (John Coltrane, Sonny Rollins, Yusaf Lateef) and jazz tunes ("Donna Lee," "Night in Tunisia"). Also, there is a reference to the effect of marijuana on M. C.'s perception of the music he listens to.

93. Zane, Maitland. *Easy Living*. New York: Dial, 1959.

Harry Steiner, an American expatriate sax player now living in Paris, narrates his experiences with several women and the difficulty he has keeping clean from drugs, one of the reasons he left the United States. The jazz content is slight, but there are several references to Charlie Parker and hard bop. The characters are pseudo-Beat bohemian types with drug and relationship problems. In the end, Harry returns to the United States and will attempt to get back into music.

DRAMA

94. Ballantyne, Bill. *The Al Cornell Story: A Comedy in Two Acts.* Toronto: Playwrights Canada, 1984.

A short, four-character play. The central character, Al Cornell, is all talk and no action. He plays piano in piano bars, discusses trivia with his less than intellectual friend, Johnny, and throws around the names of famous jazz musicians. But when the chance comes to audition with a top band at a great salary, he never shows up.

95. Caldwell, Ben. *Birth of the Blues! New Plays for the Black Theatre.* Ed. Woodie King, Jr. Chicago: Third World Press, 1989. 37-44.

A humorous one-act play that makes fun of a white reporter interviewing the great blues singer, B. B. B. B. B. B. King, "Baddest, Black Blues Boy Ever Been Born" (38). King insists throughout that to him the blues are "tight shoes" (41). He says that his favorite blues song is Mick Jagger's "I Can't Get No Satisfaction." In the end, the reporter asks, "Having been cheated, exploited, is your music now a reflection of all the sorrowful things you've encountered, and now know about life?" King replies, "No, man, it's still about my feet" (44).

96. Kanin, Garson. *The Rat Race.* New York: Dramatists Play Service, 1950.

Produced on the stage in 1949, this play was made into a motion picture in 1959 and published as a novel in 1960. The substance of the play is the same as the novel (see item 50 in the NOVELS section).

97. OyamO [Charles F. Gordon]. *The Resurrection of Lady Lester: A Poetic Mood Song Based on the Legend of Lester Young.* New York: Plays in Process/Theatre Communications Group, 1981.

—. —. *New Plays USA, 1.* Ed. J. Leverett. New York: Theatre Communications Group, 1982. 225-288.

The author says, "I call this piece 'a poetic mood song based on the legend of Lester Young' because it does not attempt to present Lester Young's life as chronological biography or as factual 'docu-drama'" (Leverett 228). The play begins and ends in a New York hotel opposite Birdland on Young's death date and shifts back and forth in time from his youth, to being on the road, to being in the Army. Emphasized is Lester's love for music: "I only know how to love music because people always seem temporary. . . ." (287). His relationship with Billie Holiday is highlighted in the play's Second Movement, pages 273-275.

98. Price, Robert Earl. *Yardbird's Vamp. African American Review* 27.1 (1993): 79-91.

A short play that emphasizes both the development of bebop by Charlie Parker and his addictions. The cast includes: Bird, the Musician, who speaks no lines but makes sounds from his horn; Bebop, based on Dizzy Gillespie; Bigger the drummer, based on Max Roach; Cool the bassist, based on Charlie Mingus; and Trick the pianist, "Red Rodney with a different axe" (79). The play has references to Parker's early years in Kansas City and his early difficulties sitting in; playing at Birdland and in Europe; being at Camarillo; and his death. The play ends with his music being a prelude to other new jazz, with references to his playing Dolphy, Coltrane, and Pharaoh Sanders lines.

99. Rahman, Aishah. *Unfinished Women Cry in No Man's Land While a Bird Dies in a Gilded Cage. 9 Plays by Black Women.* Ed. Margaret B. Wilkerson. New York: New American Library, Mentor Books, 1986.

The setting for this play is the Hide-A-Wee Home for Unwed Mothers and Pashua's boudoir, where Charlie Parker is about to die. The problems of the unwed mothers are juxtaposed with the problems of the jazz musician as the two areas of the play switch back and forth. Parker's death is announced by one of the unwed mothers in the first scene of the play and it is her love of jazz and of Parker in particular which provides the link. As Parker dies in the spontaneous coming together of the two elements in the last scene, Wilma gives birth.

100. Robertson, Lanie. *Lady Day at Emerson's Bar & Grill*. New York: Samuel French, 1989.

Set in South Philadelphia in March 1959, four months before Billie Holiday's death. In this, one of her last appearances, she sings and tells stories of her life. Interspersed with many songs associated with her, she recounts her relationship with her mother, her marriages, her addiction, the influence of Louis Armstrong and Bessie Smith on her music, and the discrimination she faced while on the road with Artie Shaw's band. After a break in her performance for a fix, she rambles on, somewhat incoherently, revealing her desire for kids and ownership of her own club.

101. Wilson, August. *Ma Rainey's Black Bottom*. New York: New American Library, A Plume Book, 1985.

—. —. *Plays From the Contemporary American Theater*. Ed. Brooks McNamara. New York: New American Library, A Mentor Book, 1988. 411-480.

—. —. *Black Thunder: An Anthology of Contemporary African American Drama*. Ed. William B. Branch. New York: Penguin, 1992. 452-520.

A two-act play set in a 1927 Chicago recording studio. "Mother of the Blues" Gertrude "Ma" Rainey makes the band members, her manager, and the record producer wait for her past the appointed time. After she arrives, she is demanding with respect to who will participate, what arrangements will be used, and having her Coke to drink. The play makes statements about the exploitation of black artists by white promoters. While waiting for Ma and for the satisfaction of her demands, the band members engage in story telling and confrontation, especially with respect to the trumpeter Levee, who is dissatisfied with his upbeat arrangement of "Ma Rainey's Black Bottom" being rejected by Ma and, at the end of the play, his original songs being turned down by the record producer, Sturdyvant, after Sturdyvant had earlier told him that he would record the songs with a band that Levee would put together.

SHORT STORIES

102. Allen, Steve. *Bop Fables*. Illus. George Price. New York: Simon and Schuster, 1955.

Steve Allen uses the language of the bopsters to retell these well-known fairy tales: "Goldilocks and the Three [Cool] Bears" (pp. 3-13): "The Three [Mixed-Up] Little Pigs" (pp. 17-30); "[Crazy] Red Riding Hood (pp. 35-49); and "Jack and the [Real Flip] Beanstalk" (pp. 53-68).

103. Anderson, Alston. "Dance of the Infidels." *Lover Man*. Garden City, New York: Doubleday, 1959. 150-167.

—. —. London: Pan, 1961.

—. —. *From Blues to Bop: A Collection of Jazz Fiction*. Ed. Richard N. Albert. Baton Rouge: Louisiana State UP, 1990. 208-222.

The narrator, Benevolence Delaney, invites a stranger, Ronnie Johnson, that he meets in a bar to come to his place to listen to jazz records. They get high on marijuana. Ronnie goes back to New York and is later visited by Benevolence. The major scene involves Ronnie taking a heroin hit and almost overdosing.

104. Angelou, Maya. "The Reunion." *Confirmation: An Anthology of African-American Women*. Ed. Amiri Baraka and Amina Baraka. New York: Quill, 1983. 54-58.

—. —. *Hot and Cool: Jazz Short Stories.* Ed. Marcela Breton. New York: Plume, 1990. 222-228.

Female jazz pianist, Philomena Jenkins, sees white Beth Baker, whose family Philomena's parents worked for in Georgia, with a black man, Willard. At the end of a set, Beth talks to Philomena, who simply listens and tells Beth to go to hell. Beth's parents don't approve of her black friend, Willard.

105. Asher, Don. "The Barrier." *Angel on My Shoulder: Stories.* Santa Barbara, CA: Capra Press, 1985. 46-67.

What is it like to sit in for the first time in an after-hours jam session—the only white player among all blacks? The story draws attention to the jazz heritage and how the experiences of blacks differ from whites and are an integral part of what makes jazz. Black characters stress the importance of experience—paying one's dues. "The barrier" refers to that between the black jazzers and the white outsider who wants to join in. He is given a hard time, but in the end an experience with two street toughs shows he has made a dent in that barrier.

106. Austin, Alex. "Dancers." *Jazz Parody (Anthology of Jazz Fiction).* Ed. Charles Harvey. London: Spearman Publishers, Ltd., 1948. 21-26.

A surrealistic vignette evoking feelings of a world destroyed and occupied by a "she" who dances with a small "he" in a dance hall/cathedral. Very little jazz significance except that the music is referred to as jazz and blues.

107. Baker, Dorothy. "The Jazz Sonata." *Coronet* (April 1, 1937): 27-32.

Hilda Means, practicing for a piano recital of Beethoven's "Sonata in C Minor," is having problems with the pressure and getting through it. A surprise visitor, jazz pianist Archie Means, helps her inadvertently when he has her lie down to rest and soothes her by playing a slow blues, *Washboard Blues.* The story makes the point of the dilemma of the musician, like Archie, who loses his freedom to play what he feels in the context of an orchestra. Archie is like Rick Martin of *Young Man With a Horn* in this respect.

108. —. "Keeley Street Blues." *O. Henry Memorial Award: Prize Stories of 1939.* New York: Doubleday, Doran, 1939. 65-76.

—. —. *A Caravan of Music Stories.* Ed. Noah Fabricant and Heinz Werner. New York: Frederick Fell, 1947. 165-174.

Geraldine Evans, in Delinquents' Home, listens frequently to Duke Ellington on the radio and aspires to sing in his band. Her first step is her attempt to win $25 in a singing contest at the Bijou. She leaves disappointed, though she is complimented by the piano player.

109. —. "They Called It Swing." *My Favorite Stories.* Ed. Maureen Daly. New York: Dodd, Mead, 1948. 119-135.

An excerpt from Book Three, Chapter 2, of *Young Man With a Horn.* Playing a dance with Jack Stuart's Collegians orchestra, Rick Martin takes an opportunity to form a quartet from the band and do some soloing. It turns out to be well-received by the audience and the small group becomes a regular feature at future dance dates. The end result of this success is that Rick is offered a job in Lee Valentine's Orchestra, which represents the big time.

110. Baldwin, James. "Sonny's Blues." *Partisan Review* (Summer 1957): 327-358.

—. —. *Fiction of the Fifties: A Decade of American Writing.* Ed. Herbert Gold. Garden City, New York: Doubleday, 1959. 31-64.

—. —. *Going to Meet the Man.* New York: Dial, 1965. 103-141.

—. —. —. New York: Dell, 1981. 86-122.

—. —. *The Jazz Word.* Ed. Dom Cerulli, Burt Korall, and Mort Nasatir. New York: Ballantine, 1960. Rpt. New York: Da Capo Press, 1987. 83-115.

—. —. *Big City Stories by Modern American Writers.* Ed. Tom and Susan Cahill. New York: Bantam Books, 1971. 55-84.

—. —. *Literary Experience: Public and Private Voices.* Ed. John Somer and Joseph Cozzo. Glenview, Illinois: Scott, Foresman, 1971. 547-572.

—. —. *Black Writers in America: A Comprehensive Anthology.* Ed. Richard Barksdale and Keneth Kinnamon. New York: Macmillan, 1972. 729-744.

—. —. *The Short Story and the Reader: Discovering Narrative Techniques.* Ed. Thomas S. Kane and Leonard J. Peters. New York: Oxford UP, 1975. 296-322.

—. —. *Major American Short Stories*. Ed. A. Walton Litz. New York: Oxford UP, 1980. 634-661.

—. —. *The Norton Introduction to Fiction*. Ed. Jerome Beaty. Second Edition. New York: W. W. Norton, 1981. 366-388.

—. — *The Borzoi Book of Short Fiction*. Ed. David H. Richter. New York: Alfred Knopf, 1983. 23-46.

—. —. *The Short Story: 50 Masterpieces*. Ed. Ellen C. Wynn. New York: St. Martin's Press, 1983. 623-654.

—. —. *Structure and Meaning: An Introduction to Literature*. Second Edition. Ed. Anthony Dube, et al. Boston: Houghton Mifflin, 1983. 217-238.

—. — *The American Tradition in Literature*. Sixth Edition. Ed. George Perkins et al. New York: Random House, 1985. 1521-1542.

—. —. *Concise Anthology of American Literature*. Second Edition. Ed. George McMichael et al. New York: Macmillan, 1985. 2009-2029.

—. —. *Fictions*. Ed. Joseph F. Trimmer and C. Wade Jennings. New York: Harcourt Brace Jovanovich, 1985. 74-96.

—. —. *Literature and the Writing Process*. Ed. Elizabeth McMahan, Susan Day, and Robert Funk. New York: Macmillan, 1986. 311-333.

—. —. *Being and Becoming: An Introduction to Literature*. Ed. Anne Mills King and Sandra Kurtinitis. New York: Random House, 1987. 624-645.

—. —. *The Harper American Literature: Volume 2*. Ed. Donald McQuade et al. New York: Harper & Row, 1987. 2078-2099.

—. —. *Fictions*. Second Edition. Ed. Joseph F. Trimmer and C. Wade Jennings. San Diego: Harcourt Brace Jovanovich, 1989. 46-68.

—. —. *Houghton Mifflin Anthology of Short Fiction*. Ed. Patricia Hampl. Boston: Houghton Mifflin, 1989. 31-52.

—. —. *The Norton Anthology of Short Fiction*. 4th Edition. Ed. R. V. Cassill. New York: W. W. Norton, 1990. 23-50.

—. —. *From Blues to Bop: A Collection of Jazz Fiction*. Ed. Richard N. Albert. Baton Rouge: Louisiana State UP, 1990. 174-206.

—. —. *Hot and Cool: Jazz Short Stories*. Ed. Marcela Breton. New York: Plume, 1990. 92-130.

—. —. *American Literature: A Prentice Hall Anthology* (Concise Edition). Ed. Emory Elliott et al. Englewood Cliffs, New Jersey: Prentice Hall, 1991. 2026-2047.

—. —. *Moment's Notice: Jazz in Poetry & Prose*. Ed. Art Lange & Nathaniel Mackey. Minneapolis: Coffee House Press, 1993. 48-78.

Undoubtedly, the most frequently anthologized of all jazz short stories—as can be seen from the list of many books in which it can be found—and probably the most highly regarded. Alienated brothers separated by age and careers finally come together when the younger, Sonny, finally gets his older brother, who feels that playing jazz for a living is disgraceful, to be more understanding about his desire to be a jazz pianist. The importance of the blues as a reflection of the past—often in relation to suffering—is emphasized. The story contains important allusions to Louis Armstrong and Charlie Parker.

111. Ballenger, Walter. "Strand." *Chicago Review* 11.2 (Summer 1957): 19-35.

Trombonist Pork Chops, whose life is pretty much wasted, attends the visitation for a drummer named Freddy, who was killed by a white man. Ironically, Pork Chops just goes to get free food, but while there Freddy's mother lets him know that she feels he could have stopped it. However, he was not there at the time.

112. —. "When the Saints Go Marching In." *Chicago Review* 10.4 (Winter 1957): 25-39.

Park Cudahay inherits $50,000 and his parents' mansion in Worden, Ohio, and invades the town with his jazz band friends, causing near riots because of their negative influence on the town's more quiet life and the morals of the college students. In the end, most of Worden is won over when the band marches to the college and then downtown, drawing large numbers of followers. They march onto the train for Chicago, it being revealed then that Park had given the rest of the money to the college.

113. Bambara, Toni Cade. "Medley." *The Sea Birds Are Still Alive: Collected Stories*. New York: Random House, 1977. 103-124.

—. —. *Hot and Cool: Jazz Short Stories*. Ed. Marcela Breton. New York: Plume, 1990. 239-259.

Sweet Pea, a manicurist, relates her life with mediocre bass player Larry Landers, who becomes jealous when she regularly services Mr. Moody, a slick gambler. Her chief concern in life is her daughter, Debbie. She likens making love to Larry to making music together. Has references to Charlie Mingus and Ron Carter (great jazz bassists) and singers Betty Carter, Bessie Smith, Mildred Bailey, Billie Holiday, Betty Roche, Nat Cole, Joe Carroll, King Pleasure, and Babs Gonzales.

114. —. "Mississippi Ham Rider." *Massachusetts Review* (Summer 1964): 621-630.

—. —. *Gorilla My Love*. New York: Random House, 1972. 45-57.

Inez Williams, representative for a recording company, and her partner, Neil McLoughlin, try to convince Ham Rider, old-time blues singer, to come to New York and make some recordings. Because he and his family need the money, he agrees on the condition that he have control over what kinds of songs he sings.

115. Bankier, William. "The Dog Who Hated Jazz." *Ellery Queen's Prime Crimes*. Ed. Eleanor Smith. New York: Dial, 1983. 38-47.

—. —. *Hound Dunnit*. Ed. Isaac Asimov, Martin Harry and Carol-Lynn Rossel Waugh. New York: Carroll & Graf, 1987. 45-55.

Blind pianist Joe Benson takes a weekend gig in Jack Danforth's hotel piano bar. His dog Queenie, however, hates jazz and is kept in Danforth's office, where she confronts a thief and takes a bite. The bite leads to Danforth's no-good son-in-law.

116. Barthelme, Donald. "The King of Jazz." *New Yorker* February 7, 1977: 31-32.

—. —. *Great Days*. New York: Farrar, Straus, Giroux, 1979. 55-60.

—. —. *Sixty Stories*. New York: Putnam's, 1981. 354-58.

—. —. *From Blues to Bop: A Collection of Jazz Fiction.* Ed. Richard N. Albert. Baton Rouge: Louisiana State UP, 1990. 264-268.

—. —. *Hot and Cool: Jazz Short Stories.* Ed. Marcela Breton. New York: Plume, 1990. 234-238.

A parody of the cutting jam session wherein one player tries to out-improvise the others.   Here, Hokie Mokie, acknowledged King of Jazz since the death of Spicy MacLammermoor, is challenged by Hideo Yamaguchi, Japanese trombonist, who wins and is anointed new King. But, within minutes, another contest is held and Hokie regains the crown.

117. Beaumont, Charles. "Black Country." *The Hunger and Other Stories.* New York: Putnam, 1957. 213-234. (Originally appeared in *Playboy* September 1954.)

—. —. *Eddie Condon's Treasury of Jazz.* Ed. Eddie Condon and Richard Gehman. New York: Dial, 1956. 384-405.

—. —. *The Playboy Book of Horror and the Supernatural.* Chicago: Playboy, 1967. 313-337.

Drummer Hushup Paige narrates the story of Spoof Collins, trumpet player, and his influence on Sonny Holmes, whom Spoof urges to switch from saxophone to trumpet When Spoof contracts cancer, he becomes mean and kills himself. Sonny takes over the band and shows signs of becoming another Spoof, with the same dedication and drive.   "Black Country" is the title of a tune Spoof wrote..

118. —. "Night Ride." *The Howling Man.* Ed. Roger Anker. New York: Tom Doherty Associates (TOR), 1988. 417-438. (Originally appeared in *Playboy* in 1957.)

New pianist Davey Green joins Max Dailey's Band of Angels. His playing reflects the tragic death of his wife. The story emphasizes how jazz comes from one's suffering. The narrator sees the band as a group of blues men and says they play "to that piece of everybody that got hurt and won't heal up." (428) When Davey meets Lorraine, his suffering is less, but Max sees the band going downhill and strives to sustain feelings of sorrow. The story ends tragically when Davey commits suicide.

119. Biggie, Patrick. "St. Louis Blues." *B Flat, Bebop, Scat.* Ed. Chris Parker. London: Quartet, 1986. 176-84.

Cuban expatriates living in Florida had to leave behind their wealth and belongings. Thomas MacAndrew, golf enthusiast and jazz lover, has his favorite record, Sidney Bechet's "St. Louis Blues," mailed to him by the present occupant of his house, a man who has "quasi-diplomatic" status.

120. Bloch, Robert. "Dig That Crazy Horse!" *Ellery Queen's Awards: 12th Series*. Ed. Ellery Queen. New York: Simon and Schuster, 1957. 81-98.

A horror story in which Professor Talmadge, who is writing a book on jazz, takes Dorothy Daniels to The Mirror Club to hear drummer Jo Jo Jones. Dorothy gets hooked on Jo Jo and on dope, even picking up the jazz vernacular, much to the displeasure of Talmadge. She dies of an overdose in the end and the band members turn out to be quasi-vampires.

121. Bonnie, Fred. "Take a Seat, Not a Solo." *Wide Load*. Ontario, Canada: Oberon Press, 1987. 65-86.

Howard Metts, harmonica-playing dreamer of fame, sits in with Big Freda at the Blues Basin and is well-received. Freda calls him back for the second set, but he urgently needs to go to the bathroom and, drunken and confused, is forced off the stand by the sax player. Refusing to be bounced out of the place, he ends up in jail overnight, playing "Dixie" for the officers when he is released in the morning.

122. Boyce, David. "Special Arrangement." *Jazz Parody (Anthology of Jazz Fiction)*. Ed. Charles Harvey. London: Spearman Publishers, Ltd., 1948. 50-56.

Drummer Jake is forced into an illegal smuggling operation by Dan O'Shay. Though appearing in a jazz fiction anthology, this story has minimal jazz content.

123. Brand, Pat. "Headlines! Headlines!" *Jazz Parody (Anthology of Jazz Fiction)*. Ed. Charles Harvey. London: Spearman Publishers, Ltd, 1948. 5-20.

Lonnie da Silva, jazz pianist, is rediscovered after twenty-five years of obscurity and forced into a concert appearance before 3,000 jazz fans. The results are surprising.

124. Branham, R. V. "Chango Chingamadre, Dutchman, & Me." *Full Spectrum 3*. Ed. Lou Aronica, Amy Stout, and Betsy Mitchell. New York: Foundation/Doubleday, 1991. 380-392.

A science fiction/fantasy story narrated by M. E. (Mervyn Eichmann), a jazz bassist. This drug-oriented story involves a time when copies of Kerouac's *On the Road* and Ginsberg's *Howl* are at a premium and being sold at exorbitant prices. M. E. is trying to save bop player Chango, a drummer, who hangs out at the Queen of Nights club where he plays "Secret Music" that has no sound coming from the instruments of its players. A recurring faint smell of cheap perfume relates to the Queen of Night, who personifies drug use.

125. Brickman, Marshall. "What, Another Legend?" *The New Yorker* May 19, 1973: 32-33.

—. —. *From Blues to Bop: A Collection of Jazz Fiction.* Ed. Richard N. Albert. Baton Rouge: Louisiana State UP, 1990. 224-228.

A parody in which blues musicologist Arthur Mice finds and interviews 112-year-old blues legend Pootie Le Fleur in Shibboleth, Louisiana in a series of 60 hours of taped conversations. Readers who enjoy Woody Allen's style of humor will like this.

126. Brown, Beth. "Jazzman's Last Day." *The North American Review* 268.1 (1983): 16-17.

—. —. *From Blues to Bop: A Collection of Jazz Fiction.* Ed. Richard N. Albert. Baton Rouge: Louisiana State UP, 1990. 292-295.

Short-short story that Brown said was inspired by jazz trumpeter Lee Morgan. Shows the lonely life of Jimmy "The Truth" Jackson, trumpeter who is obviously tired. Key line: "[There is] no BUREAU OF THE JAZZMAN'S FATE."

127. Brown, Frank London. "McDougal." *Phoenix Magazine* Fall 1961: 32-33.

—. —. *Black Voices.* Ed. Abraham Chapman. New York: New American Library, 1968. 201-204.

—. —. *Native Sons Reader.* Ed. Edward Margolies. Philadelphia: Lippincott, 1970. 287-289.

McDougal, the only white player (trumpet) in a jazz combo seems to lack the prerequisite for playing the blues, according to the other players. But he surprises the others and plays real blues because, as they come to see, he does suffer, being married to a pregnant black woman and having faced the problems of white landlords.

128. —. "Singing Dinah's Song." *Soon One Morning: New Writing By American Negroes, 1940-1962.* Ed. Herbert Hill. New York: Knopf, 1963. 349-354.

—. —. *Afro-American Literature: Fiction.* Ed. William Adams, Peter Conn, and Barry Slepian. Boston: Houghton-Mifflin, 1970. 107-113.

Daddy-o, worker in a machine shop, likes to sing Dinah Washington songs while working, but he cracks up one day and has to be carried off by the police: "Ol' Daddy-o was sure crazy about Dinah Washington. Last few days that's all he sang: her songs. Like he was singing in place of crying: like being in the plant made him sing those songs and like finally that good buddy couldn't sing hard enough to keep up the dues on his machine and then . . . Really." The narrator finds himself singing Dinah's song in the end.

129. — "A Way of Life." *Music '59: Down Beat Fourth Annual Yearbook.* Chicago: Maher, 1959. 66-67.

Sonny Stitt's recording of "Old Folks" dominates this short story. It is played over and over again in the apartment building where a man named Charlie, who is dying, awaits the arrival of an ambulance.

130. Burnap, Campbell. "A Bit of a Scrape." *B Flat, Bebop, Scat.* Ed. Chris Parker. London: Quartet, 1986. 72-92.

Teenage schoolboys Chris, Charlie, Dave, and Mick form a jazz band, the Chris Bland Quartet. Charlie wants to be a band member because he feels it will attract Alice Goodwin to him. Not playing an instrument, he opts for a washboard. Though initially greeted with amusement and joking by those at the school dance, the band is a resounding success and in the end Charlie does get the girl.

131. Cabbell, Edward J. "The Soul's Sting." *Phylon* 30.4 (Winter 1969): 413-419.

The narrator, a black saxophonist from Biloxi, moves north to Harlem and gets a job playing with Murphy Mason and the Cold Sweats, whose ambition is to get a gig at the Apollo. Jason Thomas, a young Southerner from Alabama that he meets, causes him to miss an important audition for that important job at the Apollo when he gets into a bar fight and needs help.

132. Chandler, Raymond. "The King in Yellow." *Dime Detective* March 1938: 42-74.

—. —. *The Simple Art of Murder.* Boston: Houghton. 1950. 99-161.

This story has next to no jazz content except for an informal three-man jam session in a hotel hall. Band leader/trombonist King Leopardi is one of several people murdered in this Chandler mystery starring private detective Steve Grayce.

133. Chappell, Fred. "Blue Dive." *Stories of the Modern South.* Ed. Ben Forkner and Patrick Samway, S.J. New York: Penguin, 1986. 77-100.

Blues guitarist Stovebolt Johnson comes to the Blue Dive roadhouse looking for a job promised by one Pointy Childress, who, after three years, is no longer there. The new owner, Locklear Hawkins, refuses to hire him because he's black, but while Stovebolt awaits Hawkins's decision, he entertains patrons and is well-accepted by them..

134. Cohen, Elaine. "Blevins' Blues." *B Flat, Bebop, Scat.* Ed. Chris Parker. London: Quartet, 1986. 150-174.

Over-the-hill blues trumpeter J. A. Blevins resides in a seedy hotel and lives on cheap dry vermouth. Blevins's evening in a bar is a surrealistic meeting with an elderly drunken senator, a noxious barkeep, a repulsive whore, and Abadon Beale, a man to whom J. A. owes a mysterious debt. A nightmare about a fire in Munich which J. A. had escaped turns into a fire in his hotel. As he is put into an ambulance, Beale tells him, "Even-steven." The story has little jazz content.

135. Cohen, Octavus. "Music Hath Charms." *Dark Days and Black Knights.* New York: Dodd, Mead, 1923. 1-44.

Humorous piece about Professor Roscoe Griggers, "World's Most Greatest Colored Musician and Orkestra Leader," a con man who professes to be a great cornet player but who can't blow a note or read music. He comes into Birmingham, recruits a Jazz orchestra, and develops a competition with Professor Aleck Champagne and his Jazzphony Orchestra. Things come to an amusing head when Roscoe is forced to agree to play a cornet solo and Aleck finds out he can't play.

136. Cook, Bruce. "Just a Gig." *Michigan's Voices* Winter 1962: 13-23.

Kelly, reformed jazz trumpet player addict, now married and a father, is persuaded to play a gig with an old friend and leader, Benny Powers. He plays well, but loses control of himself when he hears that Benny had told a pushy reporter that Kelly's child had just died. Kicked out of the club, he returns home, telling his wife that it was "just a gig." The story was inspired, says Cook, by his father, a jazz trumpeter.

137. Cortázar, Julio. "The Pursuer." *End of the Game and Other Stories.* Trans. Paul Blackburn. New York: Pantheon Books, 1967. 182-247.

—. —. *Hot and Cool: Jazz Short Stories.* Ed. Marcela Breton. New York: Plume, 1990. 269-331.

A classic Charlie Parker inspired story dedicated "In memoriam Ch. P." Here Parker is a worn out saxophonist, Johnny Carter. The setting is 1950s Paris and Johnny is fighting drugs and experiencing hallucinations involving time. He is undependable. The notorious "Lover Man" Dial recording session becomes the "Amorous" recording session. But the story deals chiefly with Bruno, the jazz critic and Johnny's biographer. Bruno is finishing the second edition of Johnny's biography and is simply interested in pursuing his own financial success while Johnny, on the other hand, pursues "truth." Johnny dies just as the second edition is published, knowing that the book really doesn't adequately portray him. He tells Bruno, "what you forgot to put in is me."

138. Cotterell, Roger. "Blues For Night People." *Jazz & Blues* 2.7 (Oct. 1972): 14-15.

Jazz pianist Lou, bassist Don, and drummer Eddie find that playing real jazz from the heart is not necessarily attractive to general audiences who thrive more on commercial jazz, as represented in their hit album, "Crazy Time." The story reveals the difficulty of playing for unappreciative audiences.

139. Culver, Monty. "Black Water Blues." *Atlantic Monthly* May 1950: 34-38.

—. —. *Prize Stories of 1951: The O. Henry Awards.* Garden City, New York: Doubleday, 1951. 87-97.

—. —. *From Blues to Bop: A Collection of Jazz Fiction.* Ed. Richard N. Albert. Baton Rouge: Louisiana State UP, 1990. 128-139.

Jazz pianist "Lion" Rohrs is the only white musician in Bump Roxy's all-black band, the Famous Blues Band. The story takes place at a black dance. Bump's black vocalist/wife, Adelia, is attacked by two "ugly" white men toward the end of the dance and "Lion" sits waiting, knowing that Bump will take it out on him, an available white man. Has good descriptions of the musicians playing.

140. Cundiff, Lucy. "Trumpet Man." *Saturday Evening Post* June 19, 1954: 31+.

Highly romantic story about Dan Daly, trumpet player with lip problems, who dreams of opening his own night club. With the help of a dead trumpet legend taking control of Dan's horn, he is able to sell a song he wrote. The song becomes a hit, and he is able to open the club.

141. Dabinett, Ward. "Not Commercial." *Jazz Parody (Anthology of Jazz Fiction).* Ed. Charles Harvey. London: Spearman Publishers, Ltd., 1948. 62-68.

Godfrey Spurge, songwriter, struggles to write a commercial hit. He teams up with a "poet" for the lyrics, which leads to a surprise ending. Not really a jazz-oriented story, but rather swing-oriented.

142. Davis, Clive. "I Could Write a Book." *B Flat, Bebop, Scat.* Ed. Chris Parker. London: Quartet, 1986. 122-133.

Miles Davis asks a fan named Scott to play for him while he picks up his girl at the airport. Scott is immersed in Miles to the extent that he dreams of hearing him at a concert, meeting him, and playing for him. He spends time before the concert record browsing and searching for the largest pair of sunglasses he can find—to emulate Miles. He drops into a reverie and again imagines playing with Miles—this time the electronic, latter-day Miles.

143. Deutsch, Hermann. "Louis Armstrong." *Esquire* October 1935: 70+.

Short, "semi-fictional" account of the rise of Louis Armstrong from young waif to famous jazz trumpeter. Told in dialect, folk-tale style.

144. De Vries, Peter. "Jam Today." *The New Yorker* February 4, 1950: 34-35.

—. —. *No But I Saw the Movie.* Boston: Little, Brown, 1952. 159-163.

—. —. New York: Signet, 1959. 125-128.

—. —. *Hot and Cool: Jazz Short Stories*. Ed. Marcela Breton. New York: Plume, 1990. 48-52.

The narrator takes a Benny Goodman recording of "Sweet Sue" to a "platter party." When the host denigrates swing, he sneaks out and breaks the record. In the end he discovers he had mistakenly put the record into the pocket of his host's overcoat in the closet.

145. Douglass, Archie. "'Mrs. Hopkins Pays a Call.'" *Jazz Parody (Anthology of Jazz Fiction)*. Ed. Charles Harvey. London: Spearman Publishers, Ltd., 1948. 86-91.

A female impersonator is called upon to play the role of a bandsman's mother to help with establishing the relationship of a drummer and the leader's daughter. Not much in the way of jazz/blues content.

146. Duke, Osborn. "Oh Jazz, Oh Jazz." *Eddie Condon's Treasury of Jazz*. Ed. Eddie Condon and Richard Gehman. New York: Dial, 1956. 461-488.

Emphasizes the tough life of musicians on the road. "Trumpet Sensation" Durf Green is leaving the Bly Washburn Band to work in his father-in-law's bank. Unhappy to be leaving jazz, Durf gets drunk and is hesitant to even see his wife, Eliza.

147. —. "Struttin' With Some Barbecue." *New World Writing: Second Mentor Selection*. New York: New American Library, 1952. 87-101.

Three jazz musicians driving to Atlanta for a gig encounter a strange man and his wife at a roadside grocery/diner. They argue over putting some barbecue on a spit over the fire and escape with their lives. The music element is slight.

148. Dumas, Henry. "Will the Circle Be Unbroken?" *Negro Digest* Nov. 1966: 76-80.

—. —. *Ark of Bones and Other Stories*. Edwardsville: Southern Illinois UP, 1970. 91-96.

—. —. *Moment's Notice: Jazz in Poetry & Prose*. Ed. Art Lange & Nathaniel Mackey. Minneapolis: Coffee House Press, 1993. 178-182.

Three white intruders insist on entering the all-black Sound Barrier Club to hear a new jazz which includes Probe's playing of the rare afro-horn (there are only three in the world). They are overcome by the music's vibrations and die.

149. English, Richard. *Strictly Ding-Dong, and other Swing Stories.* New York: Doubleday, 1941.

A collection of twelve stories that all have, as the title implies, varying connections to swing music and musicians. Most have as central a boy/girl theme, with the music generally having slight significance.

150. Eskew, Robert. "Time of the Blue Guitar." *Music '59: Down Beat Fourth Annual Yearbook.* Chicago: Maher, 1959. 77-80.

Relates the difficulties of a jazz combo being able to rely on the truthfulness of its leader, Zabe. He leads them along, often without paying them, and can't be trusted. He is boastful about gigs in the works which don't materialize. In the end, his players walk out on him. The story is told by the narrator using a jazz vernacular.

151. Evans, Robert. "The Jazz Age." *Jazz Parody (Anthology of Jazz Fiction).* Ed. Charles Harvey. London: Spearman Publishers, Ltd., 1948. 27-31.

A descriptive piece that evokes the idea that the roots of jazz are experience and suffering. A nice companion piece to "There's a Great Day Coming" (see the next entry).

152. —. "There's a Great Day Coming . . ." *Jazz Parody (Anthology of Jazz Fiction).* Ed. Charles Harvey. London: Spearman Publishers, Ltd., 1948. 77-85.

Emphasizes the freedoms implicit in jazz that carry over into and represent life: what jazz means, what it represents, and where it comes from. Though it sprang from ugliness and rebellion, it tells the story of life and is totally joyous. It expresses the universal; all people can relate to it.

153. Fairweather, Digby. "The Killers of '59." *B Flat, Bebop, Scat.* Ed. Chris Parker. London: Quartet, 1986. 96-107.

The new lead trumpet player in Tommy Hall's Band is not warmly received by the former lead, Manny, and the others in the trumpet section. He is forced out of the band by a devious combination of forced drinking and unreasonable demands on his lip. These trumpet players are "The Killers."

154. Feather, Leonard. "Hi-Fi Fable I: The class treatment." *Laughter From the Hip*. Ed. Leonard Feather and Jack Tracy. New York: Horizon, 1963. 87-92.

Band leader Arnie Wilson finds a way to feature his black soloist, Jimmy Ashes, at a concert near Atlanta without the white audience realizing it. Things backfire on Arnie when he finds that Jimmy has signed with a competitor and that the contract he had signed required Jimmy's being there and playing.

155. —. "You Gotta Get Lucky." *Music '59: Down Beat Fourth Annual Yearbook*. Chicago: Maher, 1959. 73-75.

A story of a double-cross in which the road manager and trumpet player of the Frankie Wood band are bested by Frankie and the vocalist, Helene. Joe, the narrator, is directed to work out a fine system for the band members. The pot builds to over $1,000, which ends up being a stake for Frankie and Helene's future together.

156. —. and Jack Tracy. "Hi-Fi Fable II: Double Jeopardy." *Laughter From the Hip*. Ed. Leonard Feather and Jack Tracy. New York: Horizon, 1963. 115-119.

The narrator, a big band trumpet player, uses a multi-speed tape recorder to try to get a job with a well-known band. He gets the job by recording at half-speed so that the band leader believes that the trumpeter has a great high register. But things backfire on him in the end.

157. Federman, Raymond. "Remembering Charlie Parker or how to get it out of your system." *Take It or Leave It: An exaggerated second-hand tale to be read aloud either standing or sitting*. New York: Fiction Collective, 1976. N.pag.

This section of the book has reference to Charlie Parker's famed "Lover Man" session and the song itself, but here Parker is in concert, rather than in the recording studio. This is a panegyric to Parker with emphasis given to the idea that blackness is a prerogative to playing jazz. The narrator tells about lending Parker his new tenor sax at a Detroit jam session during which Bird blew a forty-five minute solo on "My Old Flame."

158. Finn, Julio. "The Blue Bayou." *B Flat, Bebop, Scat*. Ed. Chris Parker. London: Quartet, 1986. 137-145.

A hobo bluesman seeks hoodoo Papa Gil's help to make a pact with the devil "so that he would have power over music" to become "a Faust of the blues." Through this he learns that the prerequisite for playing the blues is being black and having suffered. He is told he must reject the white man's religious concepts and go back to African worship and acquire the power of the *loa* [eternal spirit]."

159. Fisher, Rudolph. "Common Meter," Part 1. *Baltimore Afro-American* Feb. 8, 1930: 11. Part 2. *Baltimore Afro-American* Feb. 15, 1930: 11.

—. —. *Best Short Stories by Afro-American Writers.* Ed. Nick Aaron Ford and H. L. Faggett. Boston: Meador, 1950. 195-213.

—. —. *Black Voices.* Ed. Abraham Chapman. New York: New American Library, 1968. 73-86.

—. —. *The Short Fiction of Rudolph Fisher.* Ed. Margaret Perry. New York: Greenwood, 1987. 137-149.

—. —. *Hot and Cool: Jazz Short Stories.* Ed. Marcela Breton. New York: Plume, 1990. 12-28.

Set in late 1920s Harlem, this is the story of a battle of the bands: Bus Williams's Blue Devils versus Fess Baxter's Firemen. Baxter pulls a dirty trick by cutting Williams's drummer's drum heads, but Williams's band beats out the "common meter of blues" in another way. The rhythms of jazz and blues are held in common through the black heritage.

160. Foote, Shelby. "Ride Out." *Jordan County: A Landscape in Narrative.* New York: Dial, 1954. 16-69.

—. —. Originally published as "Tell Them Goodbye" in *The Saturday Evening Post* Feb. 15, 1947: 20+.

—. —. *New Short Novels.* Ed. Mary Louise Aswell. New York: Ballantine, 1954. 1-52.

—. —. *Eddie Condon's Treasury of Jazz.* Ed. Eddie Condon and Richard Gehman. New York: Dial, 1956. 350-383.

—. —. *From Blues to Bop: A Collection of Jazz Fiction.* Ed. Richard N. Albert. Baton Rouge: Louisiana State UP, 1990. 46-90.

Duff Conway, self-taught cornetist, finds it difficult to stifle himself and his creativity while playing the arrangements in an orchestra. He becomes ill, returns home, recuperates, and, after beginning to play again, ends up on death row for killing a man who steals his girl and humiliates him. The story, Foote said, was somewhat inspired by Louis Armstrong.

161. Fox, Charles. "'Got the World in a Jug, Lawd!'" *Jazz Parody (Anthology of Jazz Fiction)*. Ed. Charles Harvey. London: Spearman Publishers, Ltd., 1948. 99-110.

Young cornetist Joe Dumaine is hired by Kid Defaut to play with his band on a Mississippi riverboat. Young and aspiring, Joe feels things are fine—that he has "the world in a jug." A pleasant little story with no negatives and with good descriptions of jazz musicians playing.

162. Freeman, Don. "Big City Blues." *PM Magazine* May 1943, 14: 1-4, 15: 1-4.

Simple, short-short story about a trumpet player who comes to New York to find work and finds that you take what you can get because the competition is so great for chairs in bands.

163. Garceau, Phil. "The Price of Swing." *Jazz Parody (Anthology of Jazz Fiction)*. Ed. Charles Harvey. London: Spearman Publishers, Ltd., 1948. 69-76.

Denny Fletcher, black jazz band leader, compromises his music for the love of a dancer, Brownie Berrigan. He goes commercial and "[slips] away from the tunes of his race." He loses both the girl and his once "top spot" as a jazz musician.

164. Gardner, Martin. "The Devil and the Trombone." *Record Changer* May 1948: 10.

—. —. *The No-Sided Professor, and Other Tales of Fantasy, Humor, Mystery, and Philosophy*. Buffalo: Prometheus, 1987. 115-118.

—. —. *Hot and Cool: Jazz Short Stories*. Ed. Marcela Breton. New York: Plume, 1990. 44-47.

A short fantasy involving the dilemma of good (the organist) and evil (the trombonist devil). The narrator comes home puzzled as to how to approach life's problems.

165. —. "The Fall of Flatbush Smith." *Esquire* 28 (September 1947): 44+.

—. —. *The No-Sided Professor, and Other Tales of Fantasy, Humor, Mystery, and Philosophy.* Buffalo: Prometheus, 1987. 75-79.

Parody based on the revival of Bunk Johnson. Here Johnson is Flatbush Smith, inept trumpet player who evolves into a legend via a trick played by the editor of *Hot Beat* magazine, a rival of *Blue Beat* magazine.

166. —. "Sibyl Sits In." *The No-Sided Professor, and Other Tales of Fantasy, Humor, Mystery, and Philosophy.* Buffalo: Prometheus, 1987. 123-126. (Originally published as "The Trouble With Trombones." *Record Changer* October 1948: 10.)

When the narrator, a trombonist in a jazz combo, injures himself, Sibyl, a patron, sits in and is spectacular. She turns out to be a bad oboe player with the Chicago Symphony. As things turn out, they exchange places.

167. Glaser, Elton. "Blue Cat Club." *Louisiana Literature* III (1986): 22-27.

—. —. *Something In Common: Contemporary Louisiana Stories.* Ed. Ann Brewster Dobie. Baton Rouge: Louisiana State UP, 1991. 39-51.

A nine-year-old white boy, Luther Thibodeaux, is attracted to the jazz being played (especially the playing of saxophonist Crookneck) in the black patronized Blue Cat Club and finds himself in the middle of a lovers' quarrel. He witnesses a police raid on the place and the wounding by gunfire of Crookneck by the jealous club owner's girlfriend, Thelma.

168. Greenlee, Sam. "Blues for Little Prez." *Black World* August 1973:

—. —. *NOMMO: A Literary Legacy of Black Chicago (1967-1987).* Ed. Carole A. Parks. Chicago: OBAhouse, 1987. 141-147.

Prez, a junky, steals to support his habit. He listens to jazz records while sterilizing his needle. He is called Little Prez because "he dug Lester so much." He tried to be another Prez at one time, but couldn't do it. In the end, he dies of a drug over-dose. The story has many references to Prez and Basie's men.

169. Grennard, Elliott. "Sparrow's Last Jump." *Harper's Magazine* May 1947: 419-426.

—. —. *Jam Session*. Ed. Ralph Gleason. New York: G. P. Putnam's Sons, 1958. 295-313.

—. —. *From Blues to Bop: A Collection of Jazz Fiction*. Ed. Richard N. Albert. Baton Rouge: Louisiana State U P, 1990. 104-119.

A classic Charlie Parker-inspired story based on Grennard's attendance at the famed "Lover Man" recording session. In this story, Parker is Sparrow Jones. Brought to the session by his friend Cappy, Sparrow is high on drugs and the session ends tragically when he falls apart, leaving Cappy in tears.

170. Grime, Kitty. "Seeing Her Off." *B Flat, Bebop, Scat*. Ed. Chris Parker. London: Quartet, 1986. 22-30.

Overbearing, aspiring vocalist Gennie, unknowingly succeeds against major odds. Though she lacks the support of the musicians, she gets the gig and receives good reviews. However, she is then tragically killed.

171. Hannah, Barry. "Testimony of Pilot." *Airships*. New York: Knopf, 1978. 17-44.

—. —. *Stories of the Modern South*. Ed. Ben Forkner and Patrick Samway, S. J. New York: Penguin, 1986. 203-228.

—. —. *Mississippi Writers: Reflections of Childhood and Youth, Vol. I: Fiction*. Ed. Dorothy Abbott. Jackson: UP of Mississippi, 1985. 275-98.

The narrator, drummer William Howly, and Arden Quadberry, a saxophonist, play together in a high school band. In college, they form a group called the *Bop Fiends*. William becomes deaf and goes through college that way. Arden goes to Annapolis, becomes a pilot, and goes to Vietnam. Returning with a serious back injury, he dies in surgery. The jazz content of this story is slight.

172. Holmes, John Clellon. "Chorus: Walden." *The Jazz Word*. Ed. Dom Cerulli, Burt Korall, and Mort Nasatir. New York: Ballantine, 1960. 64-80.

The first section of Holmes' novel, *The Horn*. Young saxophonist Walden Blue outplays veteran Edgar "The Horn" Pool, loosely based on Lester Young and Charlie Parker. Edgar's being bested by the eighteen-year-old Walden begins the story of the sad fate of the legendary Pool.

173. —. "Tea For Two." *Neurotica* 1.2 (1948): 36-43.

—. —. *Neurotica: 1948-1951*. London: Jay Landesman, 1981.

A dialogue between jazz trumpeter Beeker and a woman who comes into the club he's playing in.   They talk about male/female relationships. Holmes uses what he terms "the vocabulary of jazz."   Includes a paragraph describing the evolution of jazz. "Tea" here refers to marijuana.

174. —. "The Horn." *Discovery No. 2*. Ed. Vance Bourjaily. New York: Pocket Books, 1953. 84-103.

—.—. *Nugget* I.5 (Oct. 1956): 16+.

—. —. *From Blues to Bop: A Collection of Jazz Fiction*. Ed. Richard N. Albert. Baton Rouge: Louisiana State UP, 1990. 140-157.

This 1953 *Discovery* selection was the first appearance in print of a section of the novel *The Horn,* which was published in 1958. This is what became the first chapter and is the same section that was excerpted as "Chorus: Walden" in Cerulli, Korall, and Nasatir's *The Jazz Word* (see item 172).

175. Houston, James D. "Homage to the Count." *The Men in My Life and other more or less true recollections of kinship*. Berkeley: Creative Arts, 1987. 125-129.

A short piece relating the writer's shock at viewing an ineffective, age 79 Count Basie on the band stand while still regarding him as "a holy man in the realm of jazz."

176. Howard, Clark. "Horn Man." *Ellery Queen's Mystery Magazine* June 2, 1980: 54-65.

—. —. *Best Detective Stories of the Year - 1981*. Ed. Edward D. Hoch. New York: Dutton, 1981. 1-12.

—. —. *The Deadly Arts*. Ed. Bill Pronzini and Marcia Miller. New York: Arbor House, 1985. 146-57.

Out of prison after 14 years, Dix returns to New Orleans. His old friend, Rainey, tries to get him back into jazz playing his trumpet. Offered a rare old silver trumpet by club owner Gaston, Dix refuses to play, being interested only in seeing Madge Noble, the woman he went to prison for. Her shooting another lover, however, frees Dix to begin playing again.

177. Hughes, Langston. "The Blues I'm Playing." *Scribner's* May 1934:
      345-51.

      —. —. *The Ways of White Folks.* New York: Knopf, 1934. 96-120.

      —. —. *Hot and Cool: Jazz Short Stories.* Ed. Marcela Breton. New
      York: Plume, 1990. 60-78.

      Young black pianist Oceola Jones and her white patron, Mrs. Dora
      Ellsworth, have differences of opinion over musical art: jazz versus "the
      old school." Dora tries to pull Oceola into Western culture, but Oceola's
      blues roots are retained, as is her love for Pete, a medical student who Dora
      feels is destroying Oceola's future as an artist. The setting is the Harlem
      Renaissance.

178. —. "Bop." *The Best of Simple.* New York: Hill & Wang, 1961. 117-119.

      Street philosopher Simple explains to the narrator the difference between
      Be-bop and *Re*-bop. He says bebop is the authentic "colored boys" music
      because it comes from the sounds of "police beating Negroes' heads." He
      says "Bop is also MAD crazy, SAD crazy, FRANTIC WILD CRAZY—
      beat out of somebody's head!"

179. —. "Jazz, Jive, and Jam." *Simple Stakes a Claim.* New York: Holt,
      Rinehart & Winston, 1957. 186-91.

      —. —. *Dark Symphony.* Ed. James A. Emanuel and Theodore L. Gross.
      New York: Free Press, 1968. 217-221.

      —.—. *Exploring Literature: Fiction, Poetry, Drama, and Criticism.* Ed.
      Lynn Altenbernd. New York: Macmillan, 1970. 211-213.

      Simple makes a case for jazz being useful to promote integration.
      Interracial seminars should be fashioned around jazz because black and
      white would dance together and thereby be integrated—all people liking
      jazz.

180. —. "Rejuvenation Through Joy." *The Ways of White Folks.* New York:
      Alfred A. Knopf, 1934. 66-95.

      This story has slight jazz significance through the love relationship
      between the drummer and female singer in a jazz band employed by
      Eugene Lesch in his Colony of Joy.

181. Hurston, Zora Neale. "Story in Harlem Slang." *American Mercury*
LV.223 (July 1942): 84-96.

Strictly speaking, not a "jazz" story, but it incorporates a great deal of the
jazz vernacular of the time.

182. Jean-Louis [Jack Kerouac]. "Jazz of the Beat Generation." *New World
Writing: Seventh Mentor Selection.* New York: New American Library,
1955. 7-16.

—. —. *From Blues to Bop: A Collection of Jazz Fiction.* Ed. Richard N.
Albert. Baton Rouge: Louisiana State UP, 1990. 158-169.

What later became a section of *On the Road*, though in a bit different form.
Sal and Dean are in San Francisco attending jam sessions in a couple of
saloons on Market Street.   References are made to West Coast jazz
musicians Wardell Gray and Brew Moore.   A quick trip cross-country
takes them to Chicago and more jazz on North Clark Street.   The latter
part of the piece traces, in improvisatory style, the development of jazz
through the 1930s, 1940s, and into the 1950s.

183. Johns, Veronica Parker. "Mr. Hyde-de-Ho." *Ellery Queen's Awards: 11th
Series.* New York: Simon and Schuster, 1956. 106-151.

New York in the 1950s is the setting for this story of the mysterious
Marvin Duffy, jazz cornetist, and a much sought-after powder box.   The
central character, Jean, works for a jazz recording label and becomes
involved through her friend, Peg.   The story includes scenes in jazz clubs
and stereotypical references to the lives of jazz musicians.

184. Johnson, Clifford Vincent. "Old Blues Singers Never Die." *The Best
Short Stories by Negro Writers.* Ed. Langston Hughes. Boston: Little,
Brown, 1967. 414-427.

A black serviceman in Paris meets an old blues singer, River Bottom, who
his father had introduced him to years ago in Chicago via the father's old
record collection.   In conversation, Bottom reveals his faith in God as a
sustaining force in his life.   As a blues singer, he says, "I could make
people laugh if I wanted, could make 'em cry too. . . ." (422).   The young
narrator indicates that music like Bottom's, the blues, doesn't age and is
always relevant, even to the young people who at the time were enjoying
rock and roll.

185. Jones, James. "The King." *Eddie Condon's Treasury of Jazz*. Ed. Eddie
      Condon and Richard Gehman. New York: Dial, 1956. 337-349.

      About Willy "King" Jefferson, legendary trumpet player who represented
      the link between Buddy Bolden and King Oliver. Bob Reynolds records
      him and the critics and fans are generally disappointed. After coming back
      out of obscurity, he is again disregarded because he really isn't playing
      well. He dies without any great fanfare.

186. Jones, LeRoi. "The Screamers." *Genesis West* 2.5 (1963): 81-86.

      —. —. *Tales*. New York: Grove, 1967. 71-80.

      —. —. *American Negro Short Stories*. Ed. John Henrik Clarke. New
      York: Hill and Wang, 1966. 304-310.

      —. —. *Out of Our Lives: A Selection of Contemporary Black Fiction*. Ed.
      Quandra Prettyman Stadler. Washington, D. C.: Howard U P, 1975.
      69-78.

      —. —. *Hot and Cool: Jazz Short Stories*. Ed. Marcela Breton. New
      York: Plume, 1990. 260-268.

      The "screamers" in this story refer to honking sax players, reminiscent of
      Illinois Jacquet and Wardell Gray, who lead a frenzied dance out of a
      dance hall into the street and back, attracting the police, who interpret it as
      a riot and treat it as such.

187. Joseph, Oscar. "Suite for Queen." *NOMMO: A Literary Legacy of Black
      Chicago (1967-1987)*. Ed. Carole A. Parks. Chicago: OBAhouse, 1987.
      192-198.

      Thirty-five-year-old tenor sax player Steven Claire Anderson plays his
      "Suite For A Queen" in memory of his mother, Lizabeth, on a Harlem
      street while looking at the window of the apartment in which they lived
      before she and his father divorced and she moved away. His playing this
      tribute to her gives him a new sense of himself.

188. Kaminsky, Wallace. "The Sound Machine." *University Review—Kansas
      City* 31.3 (March 1965): 163-174.

      Nick, a white man, had been given an alto sax by his black Army buddy,
      Buster. Nick aspires to be as much "black" as possible because he feels he

needs to be black to play jazz. His goal is to play with the great Charlie Parker-like sax player, Les Raymond. He finally gets his chance to sit in with Les and does well, but in the process he loses his friend, Buster.

189. Kelley, William Melvin. "Cry For Me." *Dancers on the Shore*. Garden City, New York: Doubleday, 1964. 180-201.

Carlyle, the narrator, relates the visit of his uncle, Wallace Bedlow, to New York, where he is accidentally discovered to be a folk/blues singer when Carlyle and Wallace visit a Greenwich Village club. His ensuing popularity leads to a Carnegie Hall concert during which the audience, black and white together, dance and have a joyous time. The crowd floods the stage and Bedlow is found dead in their midst. Carlyle observes, "he'd taken all them people, sung to them, and made them forget who they was, and what they come from, and remember only that they was people" (200).

190. Kersh, Gerald. "The Musicians." *Eddie Condon's Treasury of Jazz*. Ed. Eddie Condon and Richard Gehman. New York: Dial, 1956. 448-460.

Jazz is not mentioned in this British story, but it is implied. The narrator attends a rehearsal of the Dougal brothers septet. After, in a tavern, Jamie tells how, as a youth, he tried to hide the ivory key that came off his teacher's prized Beckstein grand piano. Originally classically trained, they are sucked into the dance band life.

191. Knight, Damon. "Coming Back to Dixieland." *The Planet on the Table*. Ed. Kim Stanley Robinson. New York: TOR, 1986. 168-197.

The time is the future and the place is the planetary system. The blues as music still survive and are rooted in the adversity experienced by those who slave away in the mines. A group of mine worker musicians compete in a music contest and win a grant for a four-year tour of the Solar System and a return to earth.

192. Kotzwinkle, William. "Django Reinhardt Played the Blues." *The Hot Jazz Trio*. Boston: Houghton Mifflin/Seymour Lawrence, 1989. 1-99.

Set in 1920s Paris, LeBlanc the magician has lost his assistant, Loli, in the Vanishing Lady Box. He and Django's Hot Jazz Trio enlist the aid of Jean Cocteau to find her. What ensues is a surrealistic adventure with little jazz entering into the story as a whole.

193. Lee, George Washington. "Beale Street Anyhow." *Beale Street Sundown*.
New York: House of Field, 1942. 13-35.

Matt Johnson, as master of ceremonies of the yearly Carnival celebration,
campaigns to keep Beale Street from being renamed Beale Avenue. He
attempts to have his friend, Tiny, elected King of the Carnival so that he
can use a devious means to get names on a petition to save "Beale Street"
and have the King offer a proclamation that Beale Street keep its name.
Music on the street is emphasized as an important part of the Beale Street
heritage.

194. —. "The Beale Street Blues I'm Singing." *Beale Street Sundown*. New
York: House of Field, 1942. 156-176.

Joker/story teller Mushmouth is upset that he must compete with blues
songs being played at Pee Wee's establishment. He feels that the music
attracts "bad men." A contest is held and Pee Wee calls it a draw between
the comedy of Mushmouth and the music of Gatemouth, Pinetop, and the
girl singer, Frankie. An altercation follows and Mushmouth is shot in the
arm by Pinetop who, along with Frankie, is sent to jail. When they get out,
they find that Mushmouth has become a blues singer.

195. —. "The First Blues Singer." *Beale Street Sundown*. New York: House
of Field, 1942. 70-86.

Young Alberta has prospects of great success as a singer in the Western
classical tradition. Her boyfriend, Charlie, plays trumpet and infuses her
spirit with a love for the blues. She unsuccessfully tries to resist singing
the blues. Her teacher, Madame Jenkins, looks down on the blues. Charlie
can't understand: ". . . songs about peasants and barbers in Europe are
quite in order but the work-and-sorrow songs in which the feeling of a
downtrodden race has found expression are considered low-down" (77).
Alberta goes to Chicago with Charlie, gains fame, goes to Broadway, and
ends up touring Europe.

196. —. "It Happened at an Amateur Show." *Beale Street Sundown*. New
York: House of Field, 1942. 36-47.

A young black girl enters an amateur contest on Beale Street and sings
"The Ethiopian Blues," dedicating it (innocently) to her white employers,
who take offense at what they interpret as "a nasty song." She calls to
apologize, playing the game to keep her job.

197. Lombreglia, Ralph. "Jazzers." *Iowa Review* 4.1 (Winter 1984): 51-63.

—. —. *Men Under Water: Short Stories*. New York: Doubleday, 1990. 99-118.

A story with strong jazz content. The narrator's friend, Bobby, is grieving about his wife leaving him. Wanting to play, he takes the narrator to where a group is jamming. The narrator is inspired to play, solos well, and gets the idea that they should start a band. The music is presented as an expression of their troubles and as an outlet for their frustrations.

198. Lovin, Roger Robert. "Professor Latiolais' Last Stand." *Music and Sound Output* Sept./Oct. 1982: 68+.

Almost forgotten, Professor Wydell Latiolais, a Creole, is sought out in New Orleans by the narrator. It is a fantasy in which the narrator finds the professor and walks with him into the past through Storyville when Latiolais performed.

199. Lowry, Malcolm. "The Forest Path to the Spring." *Hear us O Lord from Heaven thy dwelling place*. Philadelphia: Lippincott, 1961. 215-283.

The narrator, an ex-jazz musician, retires to Eridanus, a remote area in the Pacific Northwest, to regain his health after years of hard living on the road. He and his wife lead a largely secluded and spartan life, though he does have some contact with band members who surprise him with a phonograph and then a piano. He begins to do some arranging for the band and then has thoughts of writing a symphony incorporating "the true feeling and rhythm of jazz" (266). The story has some important passages about jazz and references to some of its legendary performers, like Bix Beiderbecke, Duke Ellington, and Louis Armstrong. But the story is basically about coming to terms with one's life.

200. Mackey, Henry B. "The Phenomenal Resurgence of the Spasm Band." *Record Changer* December 1950: 8+.

Jug-Head Brown, 193-year-old jazz kazoo player, is interviewed about his past in the development of jazz. He claims to have invented it in 1867: "Had a trio with Onion Skin Jackson on cigar box guitar, Broken Nose de la Cavalier on wash tub, and myself on tin whistle. Later we added Alligator Tom Long on spoons. We really played it, man!" He claims to have invented the blues and ragtime and to have recorded under the name of Jelly-Roll Morton; also, that Gershwin stole "Rhapsody in Blue" from him.

201. Manus, Willard. "Hello Central, Give Me Doctor Jazz." *New Letters* 51.2 (Winter 1984-85): 19-28.

—. —. *From Blues to Bop: A Collection of Jazz Fiction.* Ed. Richard N. Albert. Baton Rouge: Louisiana State UP, 1990. 282-290.

Recounts the visit of Len with his friend Sol, a drug addicted jazz musician who is at Cloverdale taking a cure. Sol doubts his being able to play his bass as they head off to an inmate concert. Manus said the story is "a requiem to all those great musicians like Sol whose self-destructive tendencies overwhelmed their creative gifts."

202. Marsh, Willard. "Mending Wall." *Southern Review* V New Series, (Autumn 1969): 1192-1204.

—. —. *Scenes From American Life: Contemporary Short Fiction.* Ed. Joyce Carol Oates. New York: Vanguard, 1973. 78-88.

—. —. *Hot and Cool: Jazz Short Stories.* Ed. Marcela Breton. New York: Plume, 1990. 185-199.

Miguel, at home in Mexico, gives hospitality to two American jazz musicians who must wait for a bus. During their visit, they destroy his prized jazz record collection, and he decides that Americans are savages.

203. Martin, Kenneth K. "The End of Jamie." *Negro Digest* December 1964: 63-70.

Quiet, moody, fourteen-year-old Jamie leaves Harlem to live in the South with his uncle for a summer and stays for a year. On his return, he has changed, having learned to play the harmonica, which has now become his voice and with which he expresses his moods. He plays in a jazz combo and gets married, but he continues to be unhappy. His harmonica dominates his troubled life, but he relies on it too much to speak for him.

204. Matheson, Richard. "The Jazz Machine." *The 9th Annual of the Year's Best SF.* Ed. Judith Merril. New York: Simon and Schuster, 1964. 143-150.

A prose poem narrative in which a white man invents a machine that will "convert the forms of jazz into the sympathies which made them." The machine reveals and displays the feelings that produce the blues.

205. McCarthy, Albert J. "My Home Is a Southern Town." *Jazz Parody (Anthology of Jazz Fiction)*. Ed. Charles Harvey. London: Spearman Publishers, Ltd., 1948. 57-61.

A polemical short story dealing with the problems of race in which talented blues pianist Grant Forbes returns from the North to his home in the South, knowing he will be killed.

206. McCluskey, John. "Lush Life." *Callaloo* 13.2 (Spring 1990): 201-212.

—. —. *Breaking Ice: An Anthology of Contemporary African-American Fiction*. Ed. Terry McMillan. New York: Viking, 1990. 418-432.

Earl Ferguson, leader of "America's Greatest Band," and Billy Cox, his composer and arranger, travel ahead of the band bus to the next gig. Their conversation gives insight into what their concerns are as they travel, from women to arranging new tunes to past road experiences.

207. McMartin, Sean. "Music for One Hand Only." *Phylon* 2 (Summer 1969): 197-202.

In this story most blacks have left the United States and England to return to Africa after "mysterious plagues" have destroyed most black Africans. Bernie McCafferty now sees his life changed as he seeks out no longer available jazz recordings and black football players. The few remaining blacks must guard against those who now want what was produced by blacks, like recordings by Billie Holiday and Ella Fitzgerald.

208. McSiegel, Professor Snotty [Leonard Feather]. "Bass Is Basic Basis of Basie." *Metronome* April 1944: 26.

See item 216.

209. —. "Be-bop? I Was Pre-bop!" *Metronome* December 1948: 24.

See item 216.

210. —. "I Invented Jazz Concerts." *Laughter from the Hip*. Ed. Leonard Feather and Jack Tracy. New York: Horizon, 1963. 101-107.

—. —. *From Blues to Bop: A Collection of Jazz Fiction*. Ed. Richard N. Albert. Baton Rouge: Louisiana State UP, 1990. 120-126.

See item 216.

211. —. "I Invented Bossa Nova!" in Feather and Tracy, 163-167.

    See item 216.

212. —. "Le Jazz Hep." *Metronome* June 1943: 15, 32; July 1943: 17, 31;
    August 1943: 15; September 1943: 18; November 1943, December 1943:
    19, January 1944: 30; February 1944: 20,29; March 1944: 24, April, 1944:
    26.

    See item 216.

213. —. "McSiegel Blind at Christmas: Metronome's Hindmost Authority
    Returns to Take Special St. Nicksiegeland-Type Test." *Metronome*
    January 1951: 20-21.

    See item 216.

214. —. "McSiegel's Method." *Metronome* June 1945: 11.

    See item 216.

215. —. "Professor McSiegel Tells About Sax!" *Metronome* October 1943:
    44-45.

    See item 216.

216. —. "Slide, Snotty, Slide." *Metronome* December 1943: 19.

    All of these short McSiegel pieces (items 208 through 216) are parodies.
    McSiegel is a know-it-all who claims credit for just about anything in the
    area of jazz and big band music. If something is popular, he is the one
    who started it all, from bebop to bossa nova to jazz concerts. For instance,
    "Le Jazz Hep" is a series of ten short parodies. Professor McSiegel lectures
    on the development of jazz and the history and character of the instruments
    (piano, drums, trumpet, trombone, strings) and singers. Here is an
    example of Feather's style, from the July 1943 selection: "Exercise for the
    month: Go to at least three jam sessions; make notes on everything you see,
    hear, and smell; report your findings to the nearest police station."

217. Merril, Judith. "Muted Hunger." *The Saint Mystery Magazine* October
    1963: 51-63.

    —. —. *The Saint Magazine Reader.* Ed. Leslie Charteris and Hans
    Santesson. Garden City, New York: Doubleday, 1966. 197-212.

The narrator of this mystery story is the wife of a detective. She uses her insights to solve the mystery of who it was who assaulted the tease, Cindy, a woman who hung around the Golden Horn listening to jazz and flirting with the musicians.

218. Miller, Fred. *Gutbucket and Gossamer: A Short Story.* Yonkers, New York: Alicat Bookshop Press, 1950.

A long (twenty-eight-page) short story. The time is July 1940. Teddy, the narrator, and his friend, George, their wives being out of town, get together to listen to records. After going out for seafood, George takes Teddy along on a date with a girl named Lee. Through an evening of drinking and listening to jazz, he falls for her, but she doesn't care to get involved. The main jazz reference is to George Brunies, trombone (gutbucket) player.

219. Moody, William J. "The Resurrection of Bobo Jones." *B Flat, Bebop, Scat.* Ed. Chris Parker. London: Quartet, 1986. 1-19.

Legendary pianist Bobo Jones is inspired by tenor sax player Brew Daniels and reborn as a player after living in obscurity for over a year. Daniels had died in an automobile accident.

220. Moss, Grant, Jr. "I Remember Bessie Smith." *Essence* December 1978: 66+.

James Williams looks back with fondness to his childhood introduction to Bessie Smith via the victrola and recordings of his Aunt Grace and Miss Lily Bonner, who his mother did not like because she thought the blues were disreputable. Many years later he goes back to see a changed Miss Lily and finds that the years have wiped out the joys of hearing Bessie. The story emphasizes the timelessness of what Bessie sang.

221. Murray, Albert. "The Luzana Cholly Kick." *New World Writing: 4th Mentor Selection.* New York: New American Library, 1953. 228-243. (First version of the short story, "Train Whistle Guitar.")

—. "Train Whistle Guitar." *Dark Symphony: Negro Literature in America.* Ed. James A. Emanuel and Theodore L. Gross. New York: Free Press, 1968. 376-391. (Revision of "The Luzana Cholly Kick" by Murray especially for *Dark Symphony.*)

—. —. *American Negro Short Stories.* Ed. John Henrik Clarke. New York: Hill and Wang, 1966. 209-226.

—. —. *Fictions*. Ed. Joseph F. Trimmer and C. Wade Jennings. New York: Harcourt Brace Jovanovich, 1985. 901-914.

An itinerant blues guitarist teaches two youngsters the value of getting an education, rather than emulating him by riding the rails. This is not really a jazz-oriented story, but rather a story with a message that W.E.B. DuBois would have liked.

222. Neiderhiser, Ed. "Gone in the Air." *B Flat, Bebop, Scat*. Ed. Chris Parker. London: Quartet, 1986. 113-119.

Taking off from Eric Dolphy's idea that once played, music is "gone in the air; you can never capture it again," the narrator philosophizes the extent to which music provides the "broader scope of reality," even to the degree that one can do it by using only the mind and its memory: "As I mentally played and replayed [a new composition], refining and polishing its various parts, I found myself far beyond the conventions of human reality" (118). "In the soul was the ability to recapture and experience and re-create all that had gone in the air and to ride perpetually in that sphere of reality that I had first glimpsed so briefly so long ago" (119).

223. O'Hara, John. "The Pioneer Hep-Cat." *Assembly*. New York: Random House, 1961. 103-116.

The narrator, an elderly newpaper editor, speaks to members of the High School Press Club about music in the 1920s (before swing), concentrating on the legendary one-armed singer, Red Watson. Red drank himself to an early death at age 25, an undependable pioneer in the field of jazz.

224. Oliver, Chad. "Didn't He Ramble." *Best Science-Fiction Stories and Novels*. 9th Series. Ed. T. E. Dikty. Chicago: Advent, 1958. 85-96.

A science-fiction fantasy in which wealthy old Theodor Pearsall listens to jazz played 200 years earlier. His wife, Laura, forces him to host a party, but he would rather listen to jazz. He arranges his own disappearance, contracting to be transported back in time to 1917 Storyville and the jazz world of Bunk Johnson, Kid Ory, and others. He dies as Storyville closes and has a New Orleans-style funeral parade with the band playing "Didn't He Ramble."

225. Painter, Pamela. "The Next Time I Meet Buddy Rich." *North American Review* 264 (Spring 1979): 30-34.

—. —. *Getting to Know the Weather*. Urbana: U Illinois P, 1985. 1-12

—. —. *From Blues to Bop: A Collection of Jazz Fiction*. Ed. Richard N. Albert. Baton Rouge: Louisiana State UP, 1990. 270-281.

Tony, a drummer inspired by Buddy Rich, dedicates his life to finding out what it must be like to be as talented as Buddy and to be admired as he is. In the end, he gives up his girlfriend, Gretel, for a career on the road.

226. Perlongo, Robert A. "Jollity on a Treadmill." *Jazz 1959: The Metronome Yearbook, 1959*. Ed. Bill Coss. New York: Metronome Corp., 1959. 59-61.

A surrealistic story in which sensitive, innocent Young Teddy, a student, visits Sams in the French Quarter, coming in as the jazz is getting hot and the patrons are getting raucous. Having been studying the Lost Generation, he imagines spotting F. Scott and Zelda Fitzgerald. He leaves, returns with a machine gun and kills most of the customers, but they revive and the celebration continues.

227. Petry, Ann. "Solo on the Drums." *The Magazine of the Year*. New York: Associated Magazine, 1947. 105-110.

—. —. *American Negro Short Stories*. Ed. John Hendrik Clarke. New York: Hill and Wang, 1966. 165-169.

—. —. *Miss Muriel and Other Stories*. New York: Houghton Mifflin, 1971.

—. —. *Hot and Cool: Jazz Short Stories*. Ed. Marcela Breton. New York: Plume, 1990. 53-59.

A good example of the "meaning of the blues." The main character, Kid Jones, is a drummer whose wife has left him for the piano player. His great drum solo reflects his current and past problems and is like the playing of the blues, though the audience doesn't realize this.

228. Phillips, Freeman. "Little Nooley's Blues." *American Mercury* 72.327 (March 1951): 281-292.

—. —. *Negro Digest* 9 (June 1951): 78-86.

Recounts Nooley Jackson's dramatic reaction to the death of jazz trombonist Buck Manos. He loses his ability to play his trumpet and goes about the city mourning Buck's death, unable to play. Finally, he goes to Buck's grave and is able to play there with other members of Eddie Street's Chicago Seven. The story seems to be a tribute to the New Orleans style of jazz and the insistence of those who play it that it be kept alive, even after the death of some of its best players. Bebop is implied: "The style [Buck] blew went out with button shoes" (288-89).

229. Powers, J. F. "He Don't Plant Cotton." *Accent* III (Winter 1943): 106-113.

—. —. *Primer For White Folks.* Ed. Bucklin Moon. Garden City, New York: Doubleday, Doran, 1945. 236-245.

—. —. *Prince of Darkness and Other Stories.* New York: Doubleday, 1947. 101-117.

—. —. *From Blues to Bop: A Collection of Jazz Fiction.* Ed. Richard N. Albert. Baton Rouge: Louisiana State UP, 1990. 92-102.

—. —. *Hot and Cool: Jazz Short Stories.* Ed. Marcela Breton. New York: Plume, 1990. 79-91.

—. —. *Moment's Notice: Jazz in Poetry & Prose.* Ed. Art Lange & Nathaniel Mackey. Minneapolis: Coffee House Press, 1993. 23-32.

Depicts the plight of jazz musicians who have to cater to the requests of audience members who want anything but jazz (novelty songs, hokey standards). ". . . always you wanted to play the music you were born to, blue or fast, music that had no name. You managed somehow to play that, too, when there was a lull or the place was empty and you had to stay until 4 A. M. anyway." In this story, black musicians are forced into wearing the mask for some bigoted drunken white patrons who insist on hearing "Ol' Man River." Baby, Libby, and Dodo will be pushed just so far and in the end they quit and walk out.

230. Rainer, Dachine. "The Party." *New World Writing 12.* New York: New American Library, 1957. 174-206.

The setting is a 1950s Greenwich Village party. Narrated by the hostess, it has detailed character sketches and concentrates on a small band that plays both New Orleans and bebop styles of jazz, with emphasis on the latter. The hostess, bored through the evening, submits to tolerating dancing and fights, but finally is able to be with her loved one, Tom.

231. Ramsey, Frederic, Jr. "Deep Sea Rider." *Jazz Parody (Anthology of Jazz Fiction)*. Ed. Charles Harvey. London: Spearman Publishers, Ltd., 1948. 39-49.

1948 New York finds New Orleans jazz trumpeter Nubs Wilkins wearing the mask. When white jazz groupie Jean Binns leads on members of the band, the end result is a fight between Nubs and clarinetist Arsene.

232. Roelants, Maurice. "The Jazz Player." Trans. Jo Mayo. *Harvest of the Lowlands: An Anthology in English Translation of Creative Writing in the Dutch Language*. Ed. J. Greshoff. New York: Querido, 1945. 357-375.

—. —. —. *Best World Short Stories: 1947*. Ed. John Cournos and Sybil Norton. New York: Appleton, 1947. 136-156.

Herman, a 44-year-old furniture manufacturer, allows himself two weeks per year to be a middle-aged crazy. He goes out to the Abbaye, where he hears the drummer and is inspired to take his own "leap into jazz." He gets a set of drums and a record player. Practicing by himself, he drives his wife to desperation and she breaks the head of his bass drum.

233. Russell, Charlie. "Klactoveedsedstene." *Liberator* 5.11 (Nov. 1965): 20-22.

—. —. *Afro-American Literature: Fiction*. Ed. Peter Conn and Barry Slepian. Boston: Houghton-Mifflin, 1970. 121-127.

A non-jazz story that bears as its title the title of one of Charlie Parker's famous compositions.

234. —. "Quietus." *Liberator* 4.11 (Nov. 1964): 20-25.

—. —. *The Urban Reader*. Ed. Susan Cahill and Michele F. Cooper. Englewood Cliffs, New Jersey: Prentice-Hall, 1971. 237-244.

Another non-jazz story except that it has several references to Charlie Parker and how great he was in the eyes of Randolph, a black man being used by Besso Oil to run a black gas station owner out of business.

235. Sachs, Ed. "Dogs Don't Always Eat Dogs." *Music '59: Down Beat Fourth Annual Yearbook*. Chicago: Maher, 1959. 68-71.

Remo Alberti's jazz trio is forced to share the stage with a dog act at Harry Olivetti's "Sons of Fun Niteclub." A short humorous piece that details the competition between the musicians and the owner of the dog act.

236. Salaverría, José. "The Negro of the Jazz Band." Trans. Dorothy R. Peterson. *Ebony and Topaz: A Collectanea*. Ed. Charles S. Johnson. 1927. Freeport, New York: Books for Libraries Press, 1971. 63-66.

A writer is attracted to the Negro in a jazz band playing at "The Charm of Russia" tea room. The Negro is presented as a stereotype and is in reality a white man. The story has no strong relationship to jazz, but is rather a philosophic view of life which calls for one to not get all wrapped up in striving: "Then Life becomes converted into perfect ease. Nothing upsets one, nothing presents difficulties. In a single word, one finds himself dominating Life, instead of, as in the case of most men, being dominated by life" (65).

237. Salinger, J. D. "Blue Melody." *Cosmopolitan* September 1948: 50+

The story of blues piano player Black Charles and his niece Lida Louise Jones, black blues singer. Based on Bessie Smith and her tragic death from appendicitis. Told by a man named Rudford, who knew them as a child.

238. Saroyan, William. "Jazz." *My Name is Saroyan*. New York: Coward-McCann, 1983. 90-93.

A prose poem that describes the street sounds of the city and likens them "to a kind of nervous noise that was being heard all over the country, and it was called jazz. . . ." The piece has no central jazz focus, even though its title is "Jazz." Ironically, the sounds described have no relationship to the black experience, which gave birth to jazz.

239. Scott, Tony. "Destination K.C." *The Jazz Word*. Ed. Dom Cerulli, Burt Korall, and Mort Nasatir. New York: Ballantine, 1960. 80-83.

Two railroad workers unknowingly load Charlie Parker's last remains onto a train bound for Kansas City while one of the men, Spody, makes ironic comments as he recalls meeting Bird one day and Bird telling him, "I'll be down to see you one day." Spody observes that New York doesn't treat

Kansas City cats right. Tony Scott knew Parker and played with him and continues to give him god-like admiration.

240. Shacochis, Bob. "Lord Short Shoe Wants the Monkey." *Playboy* July 1982: 116+.

—. —. *Easy in the Islands*. New York: Crown, 1985. 53-71.

This story has little jazz significance aside from the fact that a jazz club is used as part of the setting.

241. Shaw, Artie. "Snow White in Harlem." *The Best of Intentions and Other Stories*. Santa Barbara: John Daniel, 1989. 9-28.

Al Snow, aspiring jazz saxophonist, meets Eddie "The Tiger" White, an almost legendary pianist whom Al regards as the greatest. He soon gets to jam with Eddie, and what we have is another story of the old inspiring the new.

242. Shirley, Peter. "Drink and Be Merry . . ." *Jazz Parody (Anthology of Jazz Fiction)*. Ed. Charles Harvey. London: Spearman Publishers, Ltd., 1948. 32-38.

Jazz pianist Babe Sheridan's last seven days and his encounter with a mysterious blond woman who tells him she knows where his former wife Jean is. In the end he dies on the bandstand of an obvious heart attack.

243. —. "Sweet and Hot." *Jazz Parody (Anthology of Jazz Fiction)*. Ed. Charles Harvey. London: Spearman Publishers, Ltd., 1948. 92-98.

A jazzman finds difficulty coping with the idea that jazz is Art. He blames his friend, a writer, to whom he gives an exclusive story at the end by shooting himself.

244. Simmons, Herbert. "One Night Stand." *Gamma #1* (1963): 88-93.

A science fiction fantasy involving an advanced trumpet player named Maury. He places his horn above everything, even women. But when he plays a gig in Reville, his playing becomes unbelievably great when he falls for a girl, and he decides to stay there with her.

245. Škvorecký, Josef. "The Bass Saxophone." *The Bass Saxophone: Two Novellas*. New York: Knopf, 1979. 115-209.

A young jazz fan is obsessed with the idea of playing a bass saxophone with an orchestra in German occupied Czechoslovakia, where jazz is suppressed. The young boy's love of jazz, as well as the rarity of the instrument, is emphasized. The story refers to Adrian Rollini, the great bass saxophone player.

246. —. "The Bebop of Richard Kambala." Trans. Kaca Polackova Henley. *Rampike* 3.3/4.1 (1985): 101-104.

Another story with a Czech setting. Richard Kambala, after a terrific jam session with his bebop trio, commits suicide by putting a grenade in his mouth and pulling the pin. The story implies that the blues evolve from suffering.

247. —. "Eine kleine Jazzmusik." Trans. Alice Denesová. *The Literary Review* 13.1 (Fall 1969): 47-61.

—. —. *White Stones and Fir Trees: An Anthology of Contemporary Slavic Literature.* Ed. Vasa Mihailovich. Rutherford, New Jersey: Fairleigh Dickinson UP, 1977. 351-364.

—. —. *From Blues to Bop: A Collection of Jazz Fiction.* Ed. Richard N. Albert. Baton Rouge: Louisiana State UP, 1990. 230-244.

—. —. *Hot and Cool: Jazz Short Stories.* Ed. Marcela Breton. New York: Plume, 1990. 131-147.

Recounts the unsuccessful Aryan attempts in 1940 Czechoslovakia to suppress jazz by putting severe restrictions on the instruments and kinds of music musicians are allowed to play. The Masked Rhythm Bandits play music that is free and therefore symbolic of the fight for political freedom that is being waged.

248. —. "Emöke." *The Bass Saxophone: Two Novellas.* New York: Knopf, 1979. 29-114.

A story of the relationship that develops between the narrator and the Hungarian girl Emöke while he is on vacation. She is deeply spiritual and resists all men's advances. He is attracted to her and comes to love her. Aside from references to the blues, there is no significant jazz content in this story.

249. — "Song of the Forgotten Years." *New Writing in Czechoslovakia.* Ed. and trans. George Theiner. Baltimore: Penguin, 1969. 70-80.

It is 1963 and Miroslav Lavecký recalls twelve years earlier when he was in an Army band that was disciplined for playing jazz. He is in a club listening to Venci Kavan, female jazz vocalist who had sung with the Army band one evening back then. Miroslav and Venci reminisce about the past. Now the twist is popular, but Venci keeps singing jazz in a limited way during small engagements.

250. —. "That Sax Solo." Tr. Rosemary Kavan. *The Mournful Demeanor of Lieutenant Boruvka*. London: Gollancz, 1973. 25-36.

A mystery story in which police lieutenant Boruvka solves the murder of jazz band vocalist Mici Laurinov. The other characters in the story are members of the band, with emphasis given to leader Benny Polacek and tenor saxist Gustav Randal. The story has minimal jazz content.

251. Smith, C. W. "The Plantation Club." *Southwest Review* 62.1 (Winter 1977): 47-63.

—. —. *Southwest Fiction*. Ed. Max Apple. New York: Bantam, 1980. 312-329.

—. —. *Hot and Cool: Jazz Short Stories*. Ed. Marcela Breton. New York: Plume, 1990. 200-221.

Young high school musicians taken up with bebop attempt to become hip. They get caught with marijuana and have to implicate a true jazz artist, Stoogie, who ends up having to go to jail because of his second offense. The story gives a good picture of how jazz can affect the young in use of drugs, language, and dress.

252. Southern, Terry. "The Night the Bird Blew for Doctor Warner." *Harper's Bazaar* January 1956 : 101+.

—. —. *Red-Dirt Marijuana and Other Tastes*. New York: New American Library, 1967. 45-55.

Musicologist Doc Warner works on his definitive book of "the whole of Western Music." While researching bebop and the drug scene, he over-extends himself and is assaulted and robbed in an alley.

253. —. "You're Too Hip, Baby." *Esquire* April 1963: 68+.

—. —. *Red-Dirt Marijuana and Other Tastes*. New York: New American Library, 1967. 75-87.

—. —. *Hot and Cool: Jazz Short Stories.* Ed. Marcela Breton. New York: Plume, 1990. 148-161.

In Paris, white doctoral student Murray tries to get close to jazz musicians. He meets jazz pianist Buddy Talbot and his wife Jackie, who decide that Murray is "too hip" and not really sincere in forming a relationship with them. Drugs occupy a central position in this story.

254. Steig, Henry. "Gertie and the Pied Piper." *Esquire* February 1945: 44+.

Gertie, working in a pool hall, finds that jazz stands between her and Joe, the clarinetist. The story shows how musicians' lives can become dominated by jazz. Joe puts jazz before Gertie.

255. —. "Swing Business." *Saturday Evening Post* December 19, 1936: 10+.

Andy King auditions musicians for his swing band. The story emphasizes the difficulty of getting gigs and the persistence needed. The dialogue is loaded with 1930s-swing vernacular.

256. Stewart, John. "The Americanization of Rhythm." *The Black Scholar* 6.9 (June 1975): 73-77.

The narrator, a drummer in a club combo, encounters a couple, Harriet and Moses. She is much attracted to his music: "When you play I don't only have to listen, but you make me see. And the feelings . . .!" (73) She is obsessed by him. She listens to his records all the time. Invited by Moses to their apartment to have him help break the spell she is under, the narrator finds out they are Jews who wish to use him to start "a new race."

257. —. "In the Winter Of." *Curving Road: Stories by John Stewart.* Urbana, IL: U Illinois P, 1975. 82-96.

Discontented Juju can't bring himself to marry his pregnant girlfriend, Julia. Out for the evening drinking, he meets his friend Mike and they head for The Workshop, hopefully to hear Art Blakey and The Jazz Messengers. They are disappointed that Blakey doesn't show up and is replaced with a group of rockers. As they discuss their girls and their attitudes toward them, frequent references are made to jazz and legends like Coltrane. All important in the story is the idea of commitment.

258. Street, Julian Leonard. "The Jazz Baby." *Saturday Evening Post* 195 (July 15 , 1922): 6+.

—. —. *Cross-Section*. Garden City, New York: Doubleday, Page, 1923. 265-314.

Elsa Merriam welcomes her son Lindsay and his friend Chet Pollard home from college on Easter break. She is surprised to find that Lindsay has purchased a saxophone and left his cello at school. What follows is a series of boys' nights out with flappers at jazz dances, but mother, who feels that jazz is "musical Bolshevism—a revolt against law and order in music," (79) wins back her son in the end when she demonstrates her piano expertise by playing ragtime at a vaudeville show, showing up her son's jazz-baby friend, pianist Bea Morris. Lindsay opts for conservative decency over the rudeness of the flappers and decides to sell his saxophone. Overall, jazz is presented in a negative light.

259. Summers, Barbara. "Social Work." *Breaking Ice: An Anthology of Contemporary African-American Fiction*. Ed. Terry McMillan. New York: Viking, 1990. 601-614.

Alicia is facing a dilemma: should she continue to see her lover, jazz tenor saxist Richard Jones. He is an addict, and she has unsuccessfully tried to help him come clean. She throws him out, but he continues to profess his love. The story is not strongly jazz oriented; however, there is one fairly good description of an evening in a jazz club, "Giant Steps." Richard is a tenor player reminiscent of John Coltrane.

260. Sylvester, Robert. "The Lost Chords." *Eddie Condon's Treasury of Jazz*. Ed. Eddie Condon and Richard Gehman. New York: Dial, 1956. 435-447.

As an old, unnamed, renowned jazz trombonist waits to be interviewed by a jazz magazine, he imbibes Benzedrine and thinks about the development of jazz and the unglamorous life of a jazz musician, from New Orleans to Chicago to New York. There are anecdotes about Bunk Johnson and Bix Beiderbecke and life on the road, along with the new jazz innovations (bebop) and how the old school reacted.

261. Tilley, Robert J. "The Devil and All That Jazz." *B Flat, Bebop, Scat*. Ed. Chris Parker. London: Quartet, 1986. 34-38.

A devil makes a deal with a trumpet player: his soul for the ability to play hot jazz. The devil is defeated when the trumpet player switches to "cool jazz."

262. —. "Something Else." *Twenty Years of the Magazine of Fantasy and Science Fiction.* Ed. Edward L. Ferman and Robert P. Mills. New York: Putnam's, 1970. 248-262.

Dr. Sidney Williams, stranded on a small planet when his ship is wrecked, encounters a creature that is able to echo the jazz recordings that Williams plays to pass the time. He and the creature become friends, but when he is rescued, the creature is destroyed. With its unique futuristic setting, this science fiction story reinforces the idea that music is a universal language and that jazz in particular will continue to inspire and evolve.

263. —. "Willie's Blues." *Magazine of Fantasy & Science Fiction* May 1972: 54-75.

—. —. *The 1973 Annual World's Best Science Fiction.* Ed. Donald Wollheim. New York: DAW, 1972. 213-237.

A unique time-travel science fiction story in which Palmer, the narrator, travels back to the late 1930s to find the legendary jazz saxophonist Willie and play for him the famous "Willie's Blues" recording that Willie had recorded just before he died, but without identifying the artist for Willie. Willie is personally challenged to spend the rest of his short life trying to find out who the artist is and to outplay him.

264. Welty, Eudora. "Powerhouse." *The Atlantic Monthly* 167 (June 1941): 707-713.

—. —. *A Curtain of Green and Other Stories.* New York: Doubleday, Doran, 1941. 254-74.

—. —. *Selected Stories of Eudora Welty.* New York: Modern Library, 1954. 254-74.

—. —. *Thirteen Stories.* New York: Harcourt, Brace, and World (A Harvest Book), 1965. 128-40.

—. —. *The Collected Stories of Eudora Welty.* New York: Harcourt Brace Jovanovich, 1980. 131-141.

—. —. *From Blues to Bop: A Collection of Jazz Fiction.* Ed. Richard N. Albert. Baton Rouge: Louisiana State UP, 1990. 32-44.

—. —. *Hot and Cool: Jazz Short Stories.* Ed. Marcela Breton. New York: Plume, 1990. 29-43.

Welty's jazz pianist, Powerhouse, was inspired by Fats Waller, whom Welty had seen and heard when he played a dance in Jackson, Mississippi. Powerhouse is portrayed as a man of exuberance and large appetite. An important aspect of the story is Powerhouse's impromptu, fictitious story about the death of his wife and her relationship with the infamous Uranus Knockwood. The story implies much about the life of on-the-road musicians.

265. Wideman, John Edgar. "Concert." *The Stories of John Edgar Wideman.* New York: Pantheon, 1992. 213-217.

A semi-stream-of-consciousness story wherein the narrator describes a musical quartet that is similar to the Modern Jazz Quartet in terms of style and dress. He describes them in relation to his having traveled from Philadelphia into New York to hear them play. As he recalls, a friend is trying to tell him of the passing of his mother.

266. Willis, George. "Union Garden Blues." *American Mercury* 55.224 (August 1942): 176-182.

Takes place in the Union Garden and emphasizes the blues as a reflection of the problems in people's lives: here the man who cries while listening to war songs and the drunk who insists on hearing "Alexander's Ragtime Band." One of the musicians observes: "*The Union Garden Blues.* Here is where we live; here is where we are dying. Come to think of it, we *are* the *Blues.*"

267. Yates, Richard. "A Really Good Jazz Piano." *Short Story* I. New York: Scribner's, 1958. 49-70.

—. —. *Eleven Kinds of Loneliness.* New York: Atlantic-Little, 1962. 145-168.

—. —. —. New York: Dell, 1982.

—. —. —. New York: Vintage, 1989.

—. —. *Hot and Cool: Jazz Short Stories.* Ed. Marcela Breton. New York: Plume, 1990. 162-184.

Expatriate pianist Sid is in Cannes, befriended by Carson Wyler and his friend, Ken Platt. Carson is disappointed at Sid's sucking up to Las Vegas club owner, Murray Diamond.

268. Young, Al. "Chicken Hawk's Dream." *Spero* 1.2 (1966): 19-21.

—. —. *Stanford Short Stories 1968*. Ed. Wallace Stegner and Richard Scowcroft. Stanford: Stanford UP, 1968. 147-151.

—. —. *New Black Voices*. Ed. Abraham Chapman. New York: New American Library, 1972. 146-50.

—. —. *Hot and Cool: Jazz Short Stories*. Ed. Marcela Breton. New York: Plume, 1990. 229-233.

Nineteen-year-old Chicken Hawk, often drunk or high on dope, reports a dream in which he plays alto like Bird and convinces himself that he will be able to play if he gets a sax. When his friends provide him the opportunity, he fails, but blames the horn. He lives in a dream world, later telling the narrator, who sees him on a street corner, that he's headed to New York to "cut some albums and stuff."

269. Zinovy, Zinik. "A Ticket to Spare." Trans. Frank Williams. *B Flat, Bebop, Scat*. Ed. Chris Parker. London: Quartet, 1986. 58-70.

Muscovite Zinik, in Kiev for a Duke Ellington concert, finds himself caught up in a secret prayer meeting of Jews. Jazz is denoted as "forbidden fruit" because it is equated with freedom.

SELECTED CRITICISM

270. Adams, Timothy Dow. "A Curtain of Black: White and Black Jazz Style in 'Powerhouse.'" *Notes on Mississippi Writers* 10 (1977): 57-61.

Analyzes "Powerhouse" in relation to the differences in black and white jazz styles, noting the difference between Powerhouse's performance at the all-white dance as opposed to his performance among blacks during his intermission at the World Cafe. Adams also draws attention to "Black innovators of blues and jazz [resenting] the appropriation and simplification of their music by whites" (58). Uranus Knockwood is said to represent "all of the white jazzmen who have used Black jazz material for their own gain, coming after the Black jazz creators and following their musical trail" (60).

271. Albert, Richard N. "Bird Lives in American Fiction." *Coda Magazine* Issue 217 (Dec/Jan 1987/88): 12-13.

A brief overview of images of Charlie Parker in these American stories: John Clellon Holmes's *The Horn*; Ross Russell's *The Sound*; John A. Williams's *Night Song*; Herbert Simmons's *Man Walking on Eggshells*; William Melvin Kelley's *A Drop of Patience*; and Elliott Grennard's "Sparrow's Last Jump."

272. —. "Eudora Welty's Fats Waller: 'Powerhouse.'" *Notes on Mississippi Writers* 19 (1987): 63-71.

Emphasizes Welty's uncanny accuracy in depicting the character of Fats Waller in her fictional portrait of Powerhouse, taking note of the

similarities in his presence as bigger-than-life jazz personality, along with
the problems of on-the-road musicans and the concerns they have for loved
ones back home.

273. —. "The Jazz/Blues Motif in James Baldwin's 'Sonny's Blues.'" *College
Literature* 11 (1984): 178-85.

Closely examines Baldwin's use of jazz and blues allusions, especially with
reference to Louis Armstrong, Charlie Parker, the character Creole, and
the author's use of the popular song of the time, "Am I Blue," in the
climactic scene at the end of the story when Sonny plays the blues.

274. —. "Jazz and the Beat Generation: John Clellon Holmes's *The Horn*."
Moody Street Irregulars 20 & 21 (Spring 1989): 16-19.

Discusses how Holmes's implied references to Charlie Parker, Lester
Young, Dizzy Gillespie, Billie Holiday, and Thelonious Monk are aligned
with 19th-century literary greats Melville, Poe, Thoreau, Whitman, Twain,
Dickinson, and Hawthorne to promote the "philosophy of the beat
generation."

275. Appel, Alfred Jr. "'They Endured': Eudora Welty's Negro Characters." *A
Season of Dreams: The Fiction of Eudora Welty*. Baton Rouge:
Louisiana State UP, 1965. 137-171.

On pages 148-164, Appel refers to Eudora Welty's short story,
"Powerhouse," as her "Portrait of the Artist as a Jazz Musician"—an
answer to James Baldwin's statement, "I have always wondered why there
has never, or almost never, appeared in fiction any of the joy of Louis
Armstrong or the really bottomless, ironic, and mocking sadness of Billie
Holiday." Emphasis is given to the blues in relation to alienation,
loneliness, the search for identity, fantasy, and the death-wish.

276. —. "Powerhouse's Blues." *Studies in Short Fiction* II (Spring 1967):
221-234.

This article is essentially the same as the *A Season of Dreams* version,
above. Appel has made only slight changes in wording.

277. Baldwin, James. "The Uses of the Blues." *Playboy* Jan. 1969: 131+.

—. —. *The McGraw-Hill Reader*. Ed. Gilbert H. Muller. New York:
McGraw-Hill, 1982. 438-447.

Does not discuss the blues in relation to fiction, but Baldwin's interpretation of what the blues represent for African Americans is valuable when considering the importance of the blues in his short story, "Sonny's Blues."

278. Berry, Jason. "Jazz Literature." *Southern Exposure* 6.3 (Fall 1978): 40-49.

Berry proposes that "It's time to expand traditional notions of literary classification and broaden the boundaries of criticism and literary history to include those works with roots deep in the oral and musical patterns of Afro-Amerian life." Further, he concludes that "Jazz Literature demands a special form of criticism by inviting a synthesis of music and literature in a critical standard, a binding together of the two major language traditions [Afro-American and Anglo-American] into a self-conscious literary community, and a democratic one at that."

279. Billingsley, R. G. "Al Young's *Snakes*: The Blues As a Literary Form." *Obsidian* 4.2 (Spring 1977/Winter 1978): 28-36.

Discusses the blues as inspiration for Young's *Snakes*, which is distinguished by the "same paradoxical combination of pain and joy" that the blues express. "[The 'tough/gentle' behavior of many of the characters] is like a blues refrain repeated over and over; each variation representing an improvisation which yields a different nuance and gives new richness to the basic blues motif" (30). Folklore and folk motifs are also discussed as common in the blues and in Young's novel.

280. Bluestein, Gene. "The Blues as Literary Type." *Massachusetts Review* 8.4 (Autumn 1967): 593-617.

Deals with music in the African-American community as a part of its folklore and folksongs, commenting on its references in the writings of F. Scott Fitzgerald and William Faulkner, but then concentrating on Ralph Ellison's use of black folk culture, especially the blues, in *Invisible Man*.

281. Bolling, Douglass. "Artistry and Theme in Al Young's *Snakes*." *Negro American Literature Forum* 8.2 (1974): 223-225.

Emphasizes Al Young's characters in *Snakes* as being autobiographically authentic. Discusses how, for MC, "The rhythms of life and music can become one" (223). It is MC's resistance to drugs and his strong dedication to his music that gets him out of the ghetto.

282. Braithwaite, Edward. "Jazz and the West Indian Novel." *Bim* 11.44
     (1967): 275-84; 12.45 (1967): 39-51; 12.46 (1968): 115-26.

Promotes "the idea of jazz as an aesthetic model (a way of seeing; a critical
tool) . . ." (12.46:124). He says that "The West Indian writer is just
beginning to enter his own cultural New Orleans. He is expressing in his
work of words that joy, that protest, that paradox of community and
aloneness, that controlled mixture of chaos and order, hope and
disillusionment, based on his New World experience which is at the heart
of jazz" (11.44:279). He uses Roger Mais's novel, *Brother Man* to
illustrate his ideas.

283. Bruck, Peter. "Langston Hughes's *The Blues I'm Playing*." *The Black
     American Short Story in the 20th Century.* Ed. Peter Bruck. Amsterdam:
     B. R. Gruner, 1977. 71-83.

No writer has been more strongly influenced by the blues than Langston
Hughes, both in his poetry and fiction. Hughes preached pride in black
culture, and Peter Bruck here discusses how Hughes emphasizes young
pianist Oceola's family roots in jazz and blues to dramatize the contrast
between what her patron, Mrs. Ellsworth, conceives of as aesthetically
worthwhile and what Oceola considers to be of cultural significance.
Bruck says that the story "underlines historically the black's incipient
ethnic assertion, his pride in his race and the rediscovery of his cultural
setting" (79).

284. Bryant, Jerry H. "John A. Williams: The Political Use of the Novel."
     Critique: Studies in Modern Fiction 16.3 (1975): 81-100.

Bryant notes that Richie "Eagle" Stokes, in *Night Song*, is modeled on
Charlie Parker but is portrayed in the story as "a sacrificial Christ, who
dies at the hands of the oppressors so that others may be saved" (86-87).
He feels that John A. Williams is more interested in polemics than in jazz.
He also discusses the political aspects of *The Man Who Cried I Am*, *Sons
of Darkness*, *Sissie*, and *Captain Blackman*.

285. Burgess, Cheryll. "From Metaphor to Manifestation: The Artist in Eudora
     Welty's *A Curtain of Green.*" *Eudora Welty: Eye of the Storyteller.* Ed.
     Dawn Trouard. Kent, Ohio: Kent State UP, 1989. 133-141.

Says that "the jazz improvisations that [the title character in 'Powerhouse']
composes on the piano both accompany and suggest themselves as musical

equivalents to the performance of creating a story" (134).   Further, Powerhouse is "the single fully realized artist in [*A Curtain of Green*]" (134).

286. Burns, Jim. "Jazz and the Beats." *Jazz Monthly* January 1971: 17-22.

Burns presents an overview of the influence of jazz on the Beat Generation with references to Kerouac's *Town and the City*, "Jazz of the Beat Generation," and some of his recordings; John Clellon Holmes's *Go*; and Leroi Jones's "The Screamers." Burns also discusses the poetry of Gregory Corso, Ted Joans, and Frank O'Hara.   Fifty-two end-notes provide some valuable bibliographic information.

287. —. "Jivin' with Jack the Bellboy." *Palantir* 3 (1976): 19-23.

—. —. *Moody Street Irregulars* No. 3 (1979): 3-5.

Gives an overview of Kerouac's references to jazz *in Maggie Cassidy, On the Road, The Town and the City*, and "Jazz of the Beat Generation."

288. —. "Kerouac and Jazz." *Review of Contemporary Fiction* 3.2 (Summer 1983): 33-41.

Explores Jack Kerouac's references to jazz musicians and styles of the late 1930s, the 1940s, and the 1950s "with a view to indicating how accurate they were, and how they were often used to heighten the mood, or to capture the tone of a particular period in his life" (34). He looks at *Maggie Cassidy, On the Road, The Subterraneans*, and "Origins of the Beat Generation."

289. —. "Modern Jazz in Fiction: A Brief Survey." *Jazz Journal* August 1968:16-17.

Brief commentary on Ross Russell's *The Sound*; Evan Hunter's *Second Ending*; Edwin Gilbert's *The Hot and the Cool*; Elliott Grennard's "Sparrow's Last Jump;" Alston Anderson's "Dance of the Infidels;" John Clellon Holmes's *The Horn*; John A. Williams's *Night Song*; Herbert Simmons' *Man Walking on Eggshells*; Maitland Zanes's *Easy Living*; Malcolm Brady's *Shake Him Till He Rattles*; Bruce Cook's "Buzz Buzz"and "Just a Gig;" and Terry Southern's "You're Too Hip, Baby."

290. Byerman, Keith E. "Words and Music: Narrative Ambiguity in 'Sonny's Blues.'" *Studies in Short Fiction* 19 (Fall 1982): 367-372.

Sees the story as "a study of the nature and relationship of art and language" and focuses "on the underlying aesthetic question" (367). Freedom comes through the communication that music affords. The past is important as it relates to the narrator's responsibility for Sonny, as the narrator promised to his mother. The story "moves within the tension between its openly stated message of order and a community of understanding and its covert questioning, through form, allusion, and ambiguity, of the relationship between life and art" (371).

291. Carruth, Hayden. "Influences: The Formal Idea of Jazz." *Sitting In: Selected Writings on Jazz, Blues, and Related Topics.* Iowa City: U Iowa P, 1986. 22-29.

Discusses the strong influence that jazz has had on his writing, especially his poetry.

292. Carson, Gary. "Versions of the Artist in *A Curtain of Green*: The Unifying Imagination in Eudora Welty's Early Fiction." *Studies in Short Fiction* 15.4 (Fall 1978): 421-28.

Emphasizes Powerhouse the character as a symbol of the artist and examines Powerhouse in relation to Welty's belief "that the artist, at the height of sophistication and civilization, enjoys a vitalizing and purifying contact with the primitive, possesses the nearly magical power to fathom and assimilate the prelapsarian condition, a power that saves him from a sterile transcendentalism" (42). He looks at "A Memory" for the most part, but says Powerhouse "comes closest to assimilating the natural innocence of the primitive with complex ironic vision of the artist. . . ." (427).

293. Cash, Earl. "*No Sambo Smiles: Night Song.*" *John A. Williams: The Evolutions of a Black Writer.* New York: Third Press, Joseph Okpaku, 1975. 47-71.

Part Three, pages 47-61, concentrates on *Night Song*. Cash sees Hillary as a mythic figure undergoing an initiation rite, an initiation into a new knowledge of self which will only come about with a knowledge and understanding of others" (51). Hillary's being thrust into a subordinate relationship with Charlie Parker-inspired Richie "Eagle" Stokes provides the context for this initiation. Cash also says Eagle represents "victimized talent gone astray" (57).

294. Challis, Chris. "John Clellon Holmes and 'The Horn.'" *Kerouac Connection* 22 (Autumn 1991): 36-38.

Mentions Kerouac's and Holmes's love of jazz and proclaims Holmes's *The Horn* "a remarkable achievement" because "Holmes wrote about jazz with the boundless excitement and enthusiasm it inspired in him" (37). Challis only briefly discusses the structure of the novel.

295. Chambers, Leland H. "Improvising and Mythmaking in Eudora Welty's 'Powerhouse.'" *Representing Jazz*. Ed. Krin Gabbard. Durham, NC: Duke UP, 1995. 54-69.

Discusses how "the nature of jazz improvising becomes exemplified and clarified in the stories Powerhouse tells about the death of his wife"(55). Chambers sees mythmaking and improvising as analogous in this story.

296. Clark, Michael. "James Baldwin's 'Sonny's Blues': Childhood, Light and Art." *CLA Journal* 29.2 (December 1985): 197-205.

Clark says that in terms of dark and light imagery in the story, Sonny's music "is consistently portrayed in terms of light imagery" (203). Sonny uses music to regain his past: ". . . music taps the very roots of existence. . . it puts the artist in touch with the fluid emotions that he has known in perfection only as a child" (204). Any kind of art "can give us some temporary relief from brutal reality" (205) and for Sonny it culminates in his playing of "Am I Blue?"

297. Cohn, Alan M. "Welty, Waller, and 'Hold Tight': A Footnote." *Notes on Mississippi Writers* 20.2 (1988): 75-77.

Looks more closely at *Atlantic Monthly*'s insistence that Eudora Welty delete her reference to the song, "Hold Tight" from the final scene of "Powerhouse" because of the sexual innuendo in that highly popular tune of the day.

298. Cook, Bruce. "Writers in Midstream: John A. Williams & James Baldwin." *The Critic* Feb.-March 1963: 35-39.

Views Williams's *Night Song* as a "failure of imagination" (taking Richie Eagle Stokes, based on Charlie Parker and "present[ing] him as nothing more than a hipster saint . . .") (37). Says that the novel's "chief virtue is its convincing recreation of the jazz ethos and atmosphere. . . ."(37). With reference to Baldwin, no jazz elements in his work are discussed.

299. Cooley, John R. "Blacks As Primitives in Eudora Welty's Fiction." *Ball State University Forum* 14.3 (1973): 20-28.

Discusses "several different aspects of the primitivism whites attribute to blacks" (25). For many whites, jazz was a sign of primitivism. Powerhouse is a primitive in the eyes of his all-white audience and for them he wears the mask. Powerhouse's invention of Uranus Knockwood is a fantasy that represents "all the fears, apprehensions, nameless terrors which can plague a man"(26).

300. Cowley, Julian. "The Art of the Improvisers." *New Comparison: A Journal of Comparative and General Literary Studies* 6 (Autumn 1988): 194-204.

Cowley focuses on the 1950s "cultural radicalism" of those who were inspired by Charlie Parker, Bud Powell, Thelonious Monk, and other bopsters. He discusses the influence of the music on the Beats at that time and, more recently, in the work of Ronald Sukenick, Steve Katz, and Ishmael Reed.

301. Crunden, Robert. "Ralph Ellison's New World Symphony." *Indian Journal of American Studies* 13.1 (1983): 45-54.

Reviews Ralph Ellison's life-long attraction to and love of jazz. He points out the influence of both jazz and the blues on the structure of *Invisible Man*, which he refers to as an extended blues. Also, he notes Ellison's fondness for Dvorak's "New World Symphony," which incorporated black folk music. He says that *Invisible Man* is like a New World Symphony, "having themes taken largely from the black community, from jazz, spirituals and blues" (53).

302. Davis, Francis. "The Man Who Danced With Billie Holiday." *Outcats: Jazz Composers, Instrumentalists, and Singers.* New York: Oxford UP, 1990. 131-141.

Mentions Holiday's "recurring apparition in novels, poems, plays, and literary memoirs"(132) and provides excerpts from Alice Adams's *Listening to Billie*, Maya Angelou's *The Heart of a Woman*, and Elizabeth Hardwick's *Sleepless Nights*. Davis also recounts the story told him by a man who says he danced with Billie Holiday one New Year's Eve when he was a young sailor. He then goes on to discuss Holiday's 1950s recordings.

303. Davis, Thadious. "From Jazz Syncopation to Blues Elegy: Faulkner's Development of Black Characterization." *Faulkner and Race: Faulkner and Yoknopatawpha, 1986.* Ed. Doreen Fowler and Ann J. Abadie. Jackson, Mississippi: UP of Mississippi, 1986. 70-92.

This paper, presented at the 13th annual Faulkner and Yoknopatawpha Conference, reviews Faulkner's exposure to jazz and blues in the early 1900s and details how the blues, especially, entered into his characterizations of blacks, first in *Soldier's Pay*. He says that it is kept in the background and that individual musicians are de-emphasized. "[Faulkner] presents the [black musician] in exaggerated, collective motion that functions within a structure of cultural fluidity and racial interaction" (78).

304. D'Haen, Theo. "John Clellon Holmes's Intertextual Beat." *Beat Indeed!* Ed. Rudi Horemans. Antwerp, Belgium: EXA Publishers, 1985. 163-171.

Emphasizes Holmes's use of Melville as a reference point for the Beat Generation's philosophy and Edgar "The Horn" Pool as a reflection of Edgar Allan Poe. D'Haen does not go into any detail with reference to the other characters and the literary epigraphs and authors that Holmes attaches to them.

305. Dick, Bruce. "Richard Wright and the Blues Connection." *The Mississippi Quarterly* 42.4 (Fall 1989): 393-408.

Notes Wright's early awareness and appreciation of the blues as a part of African American folklore through his writing of blues and blues criticism. He was a friend of record producer John Hammond and wrote a number of blues ("Joe Louis Blues," "The F. B. Eye Blues," "I Been North and East," etc.). But it is noted that the blues do not strongly enter his fiction, except as background in *The Long Dream*.

306. Ellison, Mary. "Blues in American Fiction." *Extensions of the Blues.* New York: Riverrun Press, 1989; London: John Calder, 1989. 171-218.

An extended discussion of how the blues impacts fiction: "Sometimes the rhythmic style of the blues is emulated, at others the approach is reminiscent of the blues; occasionally the role of the blues in the life of a central character is essential and revealing. The dominance of the blues is most marked when the writer is black, and most locked into the style when the writer is also a poet" (171). Includes extensive chapter notes and a bibliography.   Writers discussed include Langston Hughes, Arna Bontemps, Richard Wright, George Schuyler, Ralph Ellison, Chester Himes, James Baldwin, Amiri Baraka, John A. Williams, Sam Greenlee, William Melvin Kelley, Ann Petry, Toni Morrison, Maya Angelou, Al Young, Gayl Jones, John McCluskey, Alice Walker, Ntozake Shange,

F. Scott Fitzgerald, William Faulkner, Ernest Borneman, Stanford Whitmore, Dorothy Baker, Jack Kerouac, and Nat Hentoff.

307. Epstein, Perle. "Swinging the Maelstrom: Malcolm Lowry and Jazz." *Canadian Literature* 44 (Spring 1970): 57-66.

Malcolm Lowry's preoccupation with jazz, most notably trumpeter Bix Beiderbecke, is emphasized. Epstein concentrates on *Under the Volcano*, *Lunar Caustic*, and "The Forest Path to the Spring," but notes that "in story after story, novels, manuscripts for future stories and novels [there are] innumerable allusions to jazz which finally culminate in a discernible pattern wherein the chaos and despair in the minds of Lowry's protagonists suddenly merge into order during a brief moment of illumination and joy." Epstein goes so far as to say the reader must have "some working knowledge of Lowry's jazz background . . . in order to understand [the characters in these three stories], the conflicts presented and , in the case of *Under the Volcano*, the structure of the plot itself."

308. Felkel, Robert. "The Historical Dimension in Julio Cortázar's 'The Pursuer.'" *Latin American Literary Review* 7.14 (Spring/Summer 1979): 20-27.

A close examination of the biographical references to Charlie Parker and others which maintains that "the tale is not an independent structure [but] rather one which needs to be placed in historical context in order to divulge its full meaning" (26). Felkel relates the theme of time to Parker's playing and to his death (his 34-year-old body resembled that of a man in his early 60s).

309. Francis, William A. "From Jazz to Joyce: A Conversation with Vance Bourjaily." *The Literary Review: An International Journal of Contemporary Writing* 31.4 (Summer 1988). 403-414.

On pages 404-407, Bourjaily discusses the influence of jazz and swing on his novel, *The Great Fake Book*.

310. Friedmann, Thomas. "The Good Guys in the Black Hats: Color Coding in Rudolf [sic] Fisher's 'Common Meter.'" *Studies in Black Literature* 7.1 (Winter 1976): 8-9.

Builds on the theme of good = white and bad = black. But in this story, the good guy has the darkest skin and prizes rhythm the most. The darker the skin, the more moral the individual. The light-skinned Fess Baxter has

"straightened brown hair" and he "avoids the black elements in his jazz."
(8) Bus Williams's "rendition of the blues is genuine." (8) "What the
listeners find is true black jazz, argues Fisher, in their origin." (9)

311. Getz, Thomas H. "Eudora Welty: Listening to 'Powerhouse.'" *Kentucky
Review* 4.2 (Winter 1983): 40-48.

Uses "Powerhouse" to illustrate "an important quality of all of Welty's
work: it is dense with gesture. In it art is recognized as a form of human
action, and also a form of social interaction. It is best thought of as the
performance of the interaction between speaker and listener in a
community or within oneself" (41). Getz notes that Welty had listened
closely to Fats Waller and that "her story is the expression of that act of
listening" and that "she enters into the improvisational activity of the jazz"
(41).

312. Goldman, Suzy Bernstein. "James Baldwin's 'Sonny's Blues': A Message
in Music." *Negro American Literature Forum* 8 (1974): 231-233.

Says that "four time sequences mark four movements while the lietmotifs
of this symphonic lesson in communication are provided by the images of
sound. Musical terms along with words like 'hear' and 'listen' give the
title double meaning. This story about communication between people
then reaches its climax when the narrator finally hears his brother's sorrow
in his music, hears, that is, Sonny's blues." (231)

313. Graham, John. "Talking With Shelby Foote—June 1970." *Mississippi
Quarterly* 24 (Fall 1971): 405-416.

Transcriptions of four taped broadcast interviews of Foote by Graham on
June 19, 1970. He questions how Foote could write about jazz without
having had direct experience. Foote says he grew up in the midst of it and
liked it. He came to know the music and the musicians. In the second
interview (412-416), he discusses his inspiration for "Ride Out." Foote
also discusses jazz as communication.

314. Gyurko, Lanin. "Artist and Critic in Cortázar's 'El Perseguidor': Antago-
nists or Doubles?" *Ibero-Amerikanisches Archiv* N. F. Jg H 3 (1980):
205-238.

Gyurko explores "a constant theme in Cortázar's art—the battle between
authenticity and pretense" (208), as represented by Charlie Parker-modeled
Johnny Carter and Johnny's biographer, the jazz critic, Bruno. Bruno is

the objective writer who becomes fearful that he will be drawn into the world of Johnny's pursuit of his true self. Bruno's biography of Johnny presents him as myth—not reality.

315. Hardy, John Edward. "Eudora Welty's Negroes." *Images of the Negro in American Literature*. Ed. Seymour Gross and John Edward Hardy. Chicago: U Chicago P, 1966. 221-232.

Discusses "Powerhouse" on pp. 229-232. Hardy claims that Welty's black characters show her awareness of "the cliches of social stereotype" and that she "often deliberately sets them up as a foil to the final, intuitive recognition of the human person" (221). He says Welty "brilliantly suggests how Powerhouse's art is inseparable from this life—and how in this way he is, perhaps, the essential Negro" (230).

316. Hattenhauer, Darryl. "Verbal and Musical Rhetoric in James Baldwin's 'Sonny's Blues.'" *Estudos Anglo-Americanos* 9-11 (1985-87): 1-7.

Discusses the problems of communication betweeen the narrator and his young brother, Sonny. Verbal rhetoric between the two has been unsuc-cessful and kept them apart. In the end it is Sonny's playing the blues (musical rhetoric) that signals their understanding one another and coming together. Hattenhauer refers to the narrator as an over-protective "Big Brother" who lacks the feeling that rhetoric depends upon for effective communication.

317. Hentoff, Nat. "Jazz and the Intellectuals: Somebody Goofed." *Chicago Review* 9.3 (Fall 1955): 110-121.

Hentoff's thesis is that the American "intellectual-artist" in searching for his roots has overlooked jazz, one of our culture's "most unmistakable strains." He concludes that "In the academies, the 'little magazines,' and other centers of intellectual activity, jazz is still America's unknown, untranslated language." (121). He notes the scant attention given to the jazz influence in fiction and feels that jazz musicians have for the most part been presented as primitives. He says that Grennard's "Sparrow's Last Jump" and Holmes' "The Horn" lack the primitivism but "describe more than they comprehend" (111).

318. Inge, M. Thomas. "James Baldwin's Blues." *Notes on Comtemporary Literature* 2.4 (Sep. 1972): 8-11.

A brief note that discusses music as a metaphor "for ordering and controlling life" (9-10). For Sonny, music is salvation.

319. Jacoby, Jay Bruce. "The Music is the Massage: Teaching Baldwin's 'Sonny's Blues.'" *The English Record* (Fall 1978): 2-4.

One aspect of Jacoby's teaching "Sonny's Blues" is his emphasis on music as a means of coping with one's problems. Sonny's music is his way of reacting to his pain.   Also, the music denotes a necessary sense of communal identity that is especially linked to the Black heritage" (4).

320. Jarab, Josef. "The Drop of Patience of the American Negro." *Philologica Pragensia* 12 (1969): 159-170.

Written during the Black Power movement, the article as a whole deals with the demands of African Americans and discusses Kelley's *A Different Drummer* and *A Drop of Patience* in that context. Jarab views *A Drop of Patience* as overly-sentimental and feels that Ludlow's decision to return to his roots in the South and play only for blacks is questionable in relation to the theme of "the American Negro's search for his identity" (170).

321. Johnson, Gerald Byron. "Baldwin's Androgynous Blues: African American Music, Androgyny, and the Novels of James Baldwin." Diss. Cornell U, 1993.

Johnson calls his methodology "mythological, psychological, and musical," with an indebtedness to Carl Jung. His study has strong references to spirituals, blues, and jazz. He focuses his discussions on *Go Tell It On the Mountain, Giovanni's Room, Another Country, Tell Me How Long the Train's Been Gone, If Beale Street Could Talk*, and *Just Above My Head*.

322. Jones, Gayl. "The Freeing of Traditional Forms: Jazz and Amiri Baraka's 'The Screamers.'" *Liberating Voices: Oral Tradition in African American Literature*. Cambridge, Massachusetts: Harvard U P, 1991. 111-122.

Relates Baraka to the technical nonconformity of the Beats and their affinity for jazz. She says, "'The Screamers' is like a free-form jazz solo" (115). "Though the music itself was born out of cultural and racial dislocations and fragmentation . . . it leads the black hearer/reader to spiritual regeneration—that 'clear image'" (121). The story "provides . . . a greater feeling of fictional boundaries through its use of jazz as subject, tonal structure, and aesthetic-ethical model" (122).

323. —. "Jazz/Blues Structure in Ann Petry's 'Solo on the Drums.'" *Liberating Voices: Oral Tradition in African American Literature*. Cambridge, Massachusetts: Harvard U P, 1991. 90-98

Petry uses the "oral traditions of jazz and blues" in "Solo on the Drums." Petry "not only takes her subject and milieu from the musical oral disciplines of jazz and blues, but combines these in a musical-literary form in the mobility of her narrative, the selection and organization of events, the conflict and resolution" (93). Jones says that music and literature come together and that "the story itself is a jazz solo on drums" (95). Kid Jones becomes one with his drums and the sound comes from his emotional depths.

324. Kamboureli, Smaro. "The Poetics of Geography in Michael Ondaatje's 'Coming Through Slaughter.'" *Descant* 14.4 (Fall 1983): 112-126.

Discusses Ondaatje as both historian and geographer whose "intent is to locate [Buddy] Bolden by locating first himself in Bolden's surroundings: a geographical undertaking" (113). He says that *Coming Through Slaughter* presents a dual spatial perception which "concerns the phenomenology of a physical landscape (Bolden is real both as a musician who lived in New Orleans and as a character in the book) and a cultural landscape (Bolden's music and the influence of jazz and prostitution on New Orleans, a physical environment)" (115).

325. Karrer, Wolfgang. "Multiperspective and the Hazards of Integration: John Williams's *Night Song* (1961)." *The Afro-American Novel Since 1960*. Ed. Peter Bruck and Wolfgang Karrer. Amsterdam: B. R. Gruner, 1982. 75-101.

Though the central character, Richie "Eagle" Stokes, is a jazz musician, the central theme is racism, says Karrer. But he does go on to compare *Night Song* and these other pieces of jazz fiction: Elliott Grennard's "Sparrow's Last Jump," Charlie Parker references in Jack Kerouac's *On the Road* and *The Subterraneans*, John Clellon Holmes's *The Horn*, and Julio Cortázar's "El perseguidor." ("The Pursuer"). He also notes that "Hip talk, bohemia setting and interracial sex are . . . standard ingredients in the jazz novel" and that "*Night Song* appears as an implicit rejection and analysis of the beatnik's admiration for Charlie Parker and be bop life styles" (96).

326. —. "The Novel as Blues: Albert Murray's *Train Whistle Guitar* (1974)." *The Afro-American Novel Since 1960*. Ed. Peter Bruck and Wolfgang Karrer. Amsterdam: B. R. Gruner, 1982. 237-262.

Karrer says that *Train Whistle Guitar* "[develops] a black fictional approach based on black folklore and the blues" (244). He goes into detail to show how "The blues permeate the novel from its title on down" (245) and how the novel is filled with "blues language" and "shares some of the basic structures and devices with the blues" (248).

327. Kart, Larry. "Jack Kerouac's 'Jazz America' or Who Was Roger Beloit?" *Review of Contemporary Fiction* 3.2 (Summer 1983): 25-27.

Discusses Jack Kerouac's use of jazz in vignettes as backdrops and the connection between jazz and Kerouac's spontaneous prose approach to writing, which Kart says is "jazz-like from the inside out, whether jazz was in the foreground . . . or nowhere to be seen. . . ." (27). His discussion touches on *The Subterraneans, Visions of Cody, Desolation Angels*, and *On the Road.*

328. Kertzer, Jon. "The Blurred Photo: A Review of Coming Through Slaughter." *Spider Blues: Essays on Michael Ondaatje*. Ed. Sam Solecki. Montreal: Vehicule Press, 1985. 296-300.

Says "Art is often seen as an organizing process: the reduction of chaos to order" but that Buddy Bolden's "music is spontaneous, violent, erratic, charged with an emotion it can hardly control. [Bolden] explores chaos without reducing it to manageable forms" and is "tormented by order" (297). Kertzer sees Bolden as one of Ondaatje's characters who are "pushed to mental and physical extremes" and who "live and die with such intensity [that] they become heroic, perfect, yet typical figures" (299).

329. Kirkpatrick, Smith. "The Anointed Powerhouse." *Sewanee Review* 77.1 (Jan.-Mar. 1969): 94-108.

Eudora Welty's character, Powerhouse, represents "all men, and since the story is a correlative of the life of art, he is all artists. And he plays the piano, which by its versatility can be said to represent all instruments" (95). Powerhouse is presented as a very talented craftsman who "is driven by passion to escape from chaos into unity, into high communion with all the universe" (99). The artist is impelled by love and "The whole story is an affirmation of love's existence" (107).

330. Klotman, Phillis R. "Langston Hughes's Jess B. Semple and the Blues." *Phylon* 36.1 (March 1975): 68-77.

The call and response narrative technique of the Simple stories, along with their familiar blues themes, prompts Klotman to call Jess B. Semple "the Bluesman" (77). Simple's tales of woe echo the blues songs.

331. Koger, Alicia Kae. "Jazz Form and Function: An Analysis of *Unfinished Women Cry in No Man's Land While a Bird Dies in a Gilded Cage.*" MELUS 16.3 (Fall 1989-1990): 99-111.

Koger says that Rahmin in her play "explores the role of music in black women's lives, the place of the black musician within a society which simultaneously idolizes him and degrades him, the relationship of the music to the community as a whole, and the spiritual dimension of the music" (104). She accomplishes these things by linking the concerns of unwed teenage mothers with the concerns of a dying Charlie Parker.

332. Lampkin, Loretta M. "Musical Movement and Harmony in Eudora Welty's 'Powerhouse.'" *CEA Critic* 45 (Nov. 1982): 24-28.

Says that Welty uses jazz elements to give her prose "the musical movement and harmony of jazz itself—black jazz" (25). She claims that Welty's rhetoric shows her knowledge of jazz and concludes that jazz has become interracial and that Welty's Powerhouse delivers his message to all of mankind. She further discusses Powerhouse as a Christ figure.

333. Landess, Thomas H. "Southern History and Manhood: Major Themes in the Works of Shelby Foote." *The Mississippi Quarterly* 24.4 (Fall 1971): 321-347.

Section II of this article covers "Ride Out." Landess sees jazz cornetist Duff Conway as a tragic hero, the story having a subtle irony that links it to the folk ballad. He likens the story to Welty's "Powerhouse" in that both use jazz musicians to embody the artist and both deal with "the nature of art itself, and its relationship to the world at large" (323).

334. Lhamon, W. T., Jr. "Keep Cool, But Care." *Deliberate Speed: The Origins of a Cultural Style in the American 1950s.* Washington & London: Smithsonian Institution Press, 1990: 228-239.

In this chapter, Lhamon discusses Thomas Pynchon's use of and references to Charlie Parker, Ornette Coleman, John Coltrane, Thelonious Monk, Clifford Brown, and the classic jazz tune "Daahoud" in his novel *V* and in relation to its central character, McClintic Sphere, jazz saxophonist. Lhamon says Pynchon through Sphere creates "a complex tonal picture of a movement in avant-garde culture. . . ." (231).

335. Lobb, Edward. "James Baldwin's Blues and the Function of Art." *International Fiction Review* 6.2 (1979): 143-148.

Says "'Sonny's Blues' is Baldwin's most concise and suggestive statement about the nature and function of art, and is doubly artful in making that statement through life situations" (143). Lobb discusses the images of light and dark, silence, and shaking ("the cup of trembling"). He says "the themes of art and life converge, for the chief obstacle to our obtaining a clear view of the past, individually or as a people, is simply our preference for bad art, for the pleasant lies which the media peddle and we in our sadness desire" (148).

336. Mackey, Nathaniel. "Interview with Al Young." *MELUS* 5.4 (Winter 1978): 32-51.

Young discusses the importance of music in his writing, particularly in *Snakes*, and in the lives of black people. He grew up with jazz and played a few instruments. He says that "Listening to music, technically speaking, has taught me a great deal about the use of rhythm and silence in my writing" (36).

337. Mansell, Darrel. "*The Jazz History of the World in The Great Gatsby.*" *English Language Notes* 25.2 (December 1987): 57-62.

Looks at the *Jazz History of the World* scene in the manuscript of *The Great Gatsby* and decides that Fitzgerald's attempt to show "the *Jazz History of the World* as strange beauty and as the vulgarization of culture" (62) was not included in the published text because it was not successful.

338. Margolies, Edward. "History as Blues: Ralph Ellison's *Invisible Man*." *Native Sons: A Critical Study of Twentieth-Century Negro American Authors*. Philadelphia: J. B. Lippincott, 1968. 127-48.

Margolies says "it is jazz, and blues especially, that becomes the aesthetic mainspring of [Ellison's] writing" (130). The structure of *Invisible Man* is blues-based and springs from the narrator's playing of Louis Armstrong's "What Did I Do, to Be So Black and Blue?" "Thus each episode serves as an extended blues verse, and the narrator becomes the singer" (133).

339. Maxwell, Barry. "Surrealistic Aspects of Michael Ondaatje's *Coming Through Slaughter*." *Mosaic* 18 (Summer 1985): 101-114.

The subject of Michael Ondaatje's *Coming Through Slaughter* is the enigmatic jazz legend, Buddy Bolden, sometimes referred to as "The First Man of Jazz." Maxwell discusses the novel in relation to surrealistic art with reference to Andre Breton's *Second Manifesto of Surrealism* and *Nadja*.

340. McCluskey, John, Jr. "Healing Songs: Secular Music in the Short Fiction of Rudolph Fisher." *CLA Journal* 26 (Dec. 1982): 191-203.

Discusses the influence and uses of black music in Fisher's short stories. Besides "Common Meter," McCluskey also covers "Miss Cynthie," "City of Refuge," "High Yaller," "The Promised Land," and "Blades of Steel." In "Common Meter," he says it is "secular music [that] binds and connects an individual call of romantic distress with collective memory" (198) when Bus Williams' band must stomp and clap to provide the rhythm that Fess Baxter has sabotaged by cutting the skins on the drums of his "Battle of the Bands" opponent.

341. ——. "Two Steppin': Richard Wright's Encounter with Blue-Jazz." *American Literature* 55.3 (October 1983): 332-344.

Focuses on "Wright's relationship with Afro-American vernacular. . . . More specifically . . . his commentary on and use of blues forms and allusions in selected poems, essays, and fiction" (333). Feels that *Native Son* shows little regard for the blues tradition and that *The Outsider* "provides for sharper commentary on the blues/secular Black culture. . . ." (336). Wright's failure to incorporate more of his folk culture into his fiction is surprising since in his essays he discussed its importance.

342. Moody, Bill. "Jazz Fiction: It Don't Mean a Thing If It Ain't Got That Swing." *Journal of American Culture* 14.4 (Winter 1991): 61-66.

Moody, a drummer and a teacher at UNLV, argues that few jazz-inspired stories have the ring of truth. He has a most positive view of Baldwin's "Sonny's Blues," Baker's *Young Man With a Horn*, and John Clellon Holmes's *The Horn*. He also makes references to Flender's *Paris Blues* and Simmons's *Man Walking on Eggshells*, but looks at neither of these in any real depth.

343. Mosher, Marlene. "James Baldwin's Blues." *CLA Journal* 26 (Sep. 82): 112-124.

Reveals how the blues informs not only "Sonny's Blues," but also *The Amen Corner*, *Blues for Mister Charlie*, *Another Country*, and *If Beale Street Could Talk*. Mosher says that Baldwin's blacks "are presented as being victimized by most whites" and that "those who do survive draw both understanding and strength from the black American blues."

344. ——. "Baldwin's 'Sonny's Blues.'" *Explicator* 40.4 (Summer 1982): 59.

Says that the narrator's sending Sonny the Scotch and milk drink at the end of the story alludes to the "very cup of trembling" passage from Isaiah 51:17-22 and signifies Sonny's conquering drugs and the narrator's acceptance of Sonny's freedom to pursue his own goals.

345. Mundwiler, Leslie. *"Coming Through Slaughter* and Tragic Bathos." *Michael Ondaatje: Word, Image, Imagination.* Vancouver: Talonbooks, 1984. 103-113.

Focuses on Ondaatje's treatment of Buddy Bolden as a bathetic character. Further, Mundwiler says, "It is futile to find, among the elements of [Ondaatje's] narrative, something which 'explains' Bolden, even something which explains jazz and the jazz artist" (107).

346. Murray, Donald C. "James Baldwin's 'Sonny's Blues'" : Complicated and Simple." *Studies in Short Fiction* 14 (1977): 353-357.

Discusses "Sonny's Blues" as a story of man's search for "identity in a hostile society." Emphasizes Baldwin's use of light and darkness as symbols, respectively, of harsh reality and relief from reality. He also notes the cyclical organization of the story and the importance of knowing "where we are and what we've left behind" (these things being implicit in the blues).

347. O'Brien, John. "The Art of John A. Williams." *American Scholar* 42.3 (Summer 1973): 489-498.

O'Brien's 1971 interview of Williams, who acknowledges his love of jazz. He says, "What I try to do with novels is to deal in forms that are not standard, to improvise as jazz musicians do with their music so that a standard theme comes out looking brand new." Only briefly does he mention *Night Song.*

348. Ognibene, Elaine R. "Black Literature Revisited: 'Sonny's Blues.'" *English Journal* 60 (1971): 36-37.

Acknowledges that the central character is Sonny's older brother, the narrator, but that the music, the blues, represents his heritage and that in accepting Sonny's playing of the blues he becomes enlightened and no longer needs to repress his personal past.

349. Ogren, Kathy J. "Controversial Sounds: Jazz Performance as Theme and Language in the Harlem Renaissance." *The Harlem Renaissance: Reval-*

uations. Ed. Amritjit Singh, William S. Shiver, and Stanley Brodwin. New York: Garland Press, 1989. 159-184.

Outlines the rise of jazz from disrepute toward respectability in the 1920s, the history and development of a jazz aesthetic, and how Claude McKay, Langston Hughes, and Zora Neale Hurston "found jazz performance helpful to the creation of an Afro-American aesthetic based on folk and working-class culture" (179).

350. Olderman, Raymond. "Ralph Ellison's Blues and *Invisible Man*." *Wisconsin Studies in Contemporary Literature* 7.2 (Summer 1966): 142-159.

Examines *Invisible Man* and shows that the story illustrates the idea that "By recognizing the meaning of the blues or gaining perception you can tear away or reverse all the conventional myths and enforced conformities until you catch sight of the principle behind them." Once done, "you must accept that you will still be free if you have accepted the fact of your humanity, your diversity." (158) The narrator's story is a blues song through which he finds his identity through experience. "Even in the Blues no one is an observer, everyone takes part, and everyone acts" (159).

351. Ostendorf, Berndt. "Anthropology, Modernism, and Jazz." *Ralph Ellison*. Ed. Harold Bloom. New York: Chelsea, 1986. 145-172.

Says that Ellison's work encompasses three frames: "(1) a ritual theory of culture and society" which "includes and structures his ideas on black folklore, (2) Modernism, which shapes his ideas of a personal and collective tradition" and "(3) . . . the world of jazz . . . [which] is understood not only as one of several discrete genres of music, but as a pervasive cultural style" (146). Further, he says, "Not only is jazz a symbolic action, it is the true musical idiom of Modernism" (147). All black music "[gives] order to the 'chaos' of black experience" (164).

352. —. "The Musical World of Doctorow's *Ragtime*." *American Quarterly* 43.4 (December 1991): 579-601.

Ostendorf feels that the emphasis put on the music by making it the title of the book indicates that E. L. Doctorow intended that Coalhouse Walker's quest for civil and human rights should parallel Scott Joplin's quest for musical respectability.

353. Reilly, John M. "'Sonny's Blues': James Baldwin's Image of Black Community." *Negro American Literature Forum* 4.2 (1970): 56-60.

—. —. *James Baldwin: A Collection of Critical Essays*. Ed. Keneth Kinnamon. Englewood Cliffs, New Jersey: Prentice-Hall, 1974. 139-146.

Maintains that "Sonny's Blues" "provides an esthetic linking [Baldwin's] work . . . with the cultures of the Black ghetto" (56) and that "the basis of the story . . . lies in his use of the Blues as a key metaphor [of the black community]" (56). He concludes, "The Blues is expression in which one uses the skill he has achieved by practice and experience in order to reach toward others. It is this proposition that gives the Blues its metaphoric significance" (59).

354. Ro, Sigmund. "The Black Musician as Literary Hero: Baldwin's 'Sonny's Blues' and Kelley's 'Cry for Me.'" *American Studies in Scandinavia* 7.1: 17-48.

—. —. *Rage and Celebration: Essays on Contemporary Afro-American Writing*. Atlantic Heights, NJ: Humanities Press, 1984. 12-27.

Emphasizes music as having a "therapeutic function and a racial core": "It functions as a means of escape from the ghetto and as a psychological buffer to this." He notes that the "universalizing formula" in "Sonny's Blues" has its roots in "contemporary existentialist thought" (24). He interprets Sonny as Absurd Man: "Such concepts as Dread (Angst), nausea, alienation, and absurd freedom sum up his isolated stance as outsider-hero with considerable accuracy" (28).

355. Robbins, Susan. "Anguish and Anger." *Virginia English Bulletin* 36.2 (Winter 1986): 59-61.

Compares James Joyce's "Araby" and James Baldwin's "Sonny's Blues" in relation to the theme, "Anger and anguish are the fires that burn away innocence . . ." (59). Sonny gains his freedom from anger and anguish through his music, through playing the blues, and his older brother comes to understand Sonny by listening to Sonny play the blues.

356. Robertson, Patricia. "Baldwin's 'Sonny's Blues': The Scapegoat Metaphor." *University of Mississippi Studies in English* 9 (1991): 189-198.

Sees Sonny as a literary scapegoat who shares his sorrow through his music. "The blues metaphor also involves suffering and the sharing of suffering that supersedes race and time and cements us all together within

our shared humanity" (190).   Sonny is the "ultimate scapegoat" who
through his music "has power to transform both his and our pain. . . ."
(190).

357. Romanet, Jerome de. "Musical Elements in *Invisible Man* with Special
References to the Blues." *Delta* 18 (April 1984): 105-118.

Explores the many allusions to music, especially the blues, in *Invisible
Man*. Says that "music is the privileged means by which the protagonist is
capable of reaching back and being reunited with his origins" (107).
Discusses, in turn, 1 - "Music as a Theme in Invisible Man," 2 - "Music as
Collective Memory," 3 - "The Literary Transcription of Two Blues
'Moods': The Mocking Bird and Poor Robin," 4 - "The Blues as Ritual,"
and, 5 - "The Quest for an Identity and Invisibility as Blues Themes."

358. Rooke, Constance. "Dog in a Grey Room: The Happy Ending of *Coming
Through Slaughter*." *Spider Blues: Essays on Michael Ondaatje*. Ed. Sam
Solecki. Montreal: Vehicule Press, 1985. 268-292.

Sees Buddy Bolden as "the hero of the novel. . . . an exemplary case of the
artist as hero" (268). Ondaatje places Bolden in the foreground while
covering the images of "landscape, rooms and wallpaper, clouds, veins, the
polarity of black and white, the colour blue, dogs, the mattress whores, and
the dolphin sonographs" (270). Rooke compares and contrasts Bolden the
musical artist with Bellocq the photographic artist.

359. Salamone, Frank A. "The Force Primeval: An Image of Jazz in American
Literature." *Play & Culture* 3.3 (1990): 256-266.

Examines Stanford Whitmore's *Solo* and Joseph Škvorecký's *The Bass
Saxophone* in relation to the jazz artist being presented "either as a darkly
romantic, tortured figure or as a force for liberation" (256). In *Solo* it is
freedom from the agents, critics, and fans to do one's own thing. In *The
Bass Saxophone* it is the freedom to play an outlawed music in Nazi-
occupied Czechoslovakia during World War II.

360. Savery, Pancho. "Baldwin, Bebop, and 'Sonny's Blues.'" *Understanding
Others: Cultural and Cross-Cultural Studies and the Teaching of Litera-
ture*. Ed. Joseph Trimmer and Tilly Warnock. Urbana, Illinois: National
Council of Teachers of English, 1992. 165-176.

Savery concentrates on the music (the blues) and Baldwin's having "gotten
to the specificities of the music and the wider cultural implications" (166).

He strongly emphasizes that music is "at the center of African American culture" and goes on to show how this is reflected in "Sonny's Blues." He also says that Bebop reflects militancy.

361. Schmidt, Peter. "Sibyls in Eudora Welty's Stories." *Eudora Welty: Eye of the Storyteller*. Ed. Dawn Trouard. Kent, Ohio: Kent State UP, 1989. 78-93.

Discusses the sibyl figure in the stories "Powerhouse," "Music From Spain," and "The Wanderers." Powerhouse as a sibyl exerts a hidden power that uses signals and code words in contrast to his white audience's exertion of power by using written texts. Powerhouse "wears the mask" and maintains his freedom and dignity as an artist. "Welty's image of Powerhouse as a sibyl altering his or her culture's texts is the single most powerful instance in *A Curtain of Green* of what she expects a heroine (and an artist) to be" (82).

362. Schmitz, Neil. "Al Young's *Snakes*: Words to the Music." *Paunch* 35 (1974): 3-9.

Schmitz says that music is the subject of *Snakes*: blues, rhythm and blues, and jazz. The central character, MC, matures through the mentoring of the junky, Champ, who tells him, "you got to learn to get on down inside yourself." MC's task is to acknowledge the past, but also to move ahead to John Coltrane, Ornette Coleman, and beyond. Schmitz says that "MC's quest for the right language in his music is a reflection of [author] Young's discovery of the music in his language" (7).

363. Scobie, Stephen. "*Coming Through Slaughter*: Fictional Magnets and Spider's Webbs." *Essays on Canadian Writing* 12 (Fall 1978): 5-23.

Scobie says, "The central subject of *Coming Through Slaughter* is the experience . . . of a certain kind of artist: beset by fame, obsessed by problems of equilibrium, ultimately self-destructive" (6). "In Buddy Bolden, the theme is tackled directly, in terms of the art form, jazz, which depends most centrally on improvisation, and in terms of a case history, a career, whose fascination stems from its drastically self-destructive conclusion" (6).

364. Škvorecký, Josef. "Drops of Jazz in My Fiction." *Black American Literature Forum* 25.3 (Fall 1991): 621-632.

Škvorecký explains how he got hooked on jazz in the early 1940s when his father gave him a wind-up record player. However, he was unsuccessful in his attempts to play tenor sax. But jazz found its way into his first novel, *The Cowards*. "All my effort went into attempts to describe and express how we, the then-young people, felt about jazz, what it meant for us, and how hard it was to come across the genuine thing in the domain of the Aryans" (625). He also touches on his use of jazz in "The Bebop of Richard Kambala," "The Bass Saxophone," and *The Swell Season*. He quotes at some length from each work.

365. Smith, Jr., Hugh L. "The Literary Manifestation of a Liberal Romanticism in American Jazz." Diss. U New Mexico, 1955.

Makes a case for jazz's indebtedness to American literature for what he recognized at that time as "its growing national recognition as an art form" (iii). His main thesis is that "all genres of the literature of Jazz have adopted an attitude of Liberal Romanticism in their treatment of Jazz" (ii), Liberal Romanticism being characterized as having the Romantic elements of "an expressive individualism, an ideal standard for both art and behavior, a belief in art approaching an art-religion, a general non-conformity to the *status-quo*, and an element of anti-materialism," along with the Liberal qualities of "a firm belief in racial equality and brotherhood, a strong sense of humor with which to meet reality, a general attitude of anti-snobbery and informality, and an implied belief in the perfectability of mankind" (ii-iii).

366. —. "Jazz in the American Novel." *English Journal* 47.8 (November 1958): 467-478.

This is one of the earliest discussions of jazz in fiction and is a shortened version of Chapter 5 of his 1955 Ph.D. dissertation (see item 365). Smith notes these three trends in novelists' references to jazz: "a quantitative increase in jazz subject matter, a qualitative advancement in the accuracy of portrayal of the jazz world, and a consistently romantic treatment of jazz subject matter." He then surveys writers as wide-ranging as Michael Arlen, F. Scott Fitzgerald, Carl Van Vechten, Du Bose Heyward, Thomas Wolfe, Chandler Brossard, Dorothy Baker, Dale Curran, Harold Sinclair, Eudora Welty, John Clellon Holmes, John O'Hara, Henry Miller, James Jones, J. D. Salinger, Evan Hunter, Bucklin Moon, and Ralph Ellison. .

367. Solecki, Sam. "Making and Destroying: *Coming Through Slaughter* and Extremist Art." *Essays on Canadian Writing* 12 (Fall 1978): 24-47.

Interprets "the novel's central character, the cornetist Buddy Bolden, as a representative figure through whom Ondaatje is examining critically both the complex nature of his own creativity and three problematic notions central to modern art: the relationship between self-destructiveness and creativity, the influence of the audience upon the artist, and, by implication, the concept of the avant-garde" (27). Says that Ondaatje's Bolden is a self-portrait.

368. Stephenson, Gregory. "Homeward From Nowhere: Notes on the Novels of John Clellon Holmes." *The Kerouac Connection* 15 (1988): 20-27.

—. —. *The Daybreak Boys: Essays on the Literature of the Beat Generation*. Carbondale, IL: Southern Illinois UP, 1990. 90-104.

Stephenson regards *Go, The Horn,* and *Get Home Free* as interrelated novels. Sees music as "a metaphor . . . for the spiritual search and aspiration of man as a vehicle of expression for certain elusive truths and for a knowledge beyond language" (102). He concentrates on *The Horn* on pages 95-98, noting that "Three interlocked clusters of images convey the thematic movement of *The Horn*: religious imagery, musical imagery, and the imagery of birds and of flight" (96). He says that the bird images apply to jazz musicians and the flight images apply to jazz music.

369. Stone, William B. "Eudora Welty's Hydrodynamic 'Powerhouse.'" *Studies in Short Fiction* 11.1 (1974): 93-96.

Emphasizes the recurrent water images in "Powerhouse," saying, "They form a pattern that draws together Miss Welty's related themes of death, reality, Negritude, and art" (94). Powerhouse "accepts water as his element, moves naturally in it, and thereby gains his strength—his power to overcome tragedy, and to produce his music" (94).

370. Szwed, John F. "Josef Škvorecký and the Tradition of Jazz Literature." *World Literature Today* 54 (Autumn 1980): 586-590.

Essentially the same article as the *Village Voice* piece (next entry), but it has additional material on Škvorecký. It concentrates on *The Cowards,* "Song of the Forgotten Years," "Emöke," and "The Bass Saxophone." Szwed concludes, "What finally is unique and appealing in Škvorecký's writing is its Europeaness, the very distance between his characters' love for jazz and the sources of the music" (589).

371. —. "Really the (Typed-Out) Blues: Jazz Fiction in Search of Its Dr. Faustus." *Village Voice* July 2, 1979: 74+.

Discusses how jazz has impacted literature but has not inspired any first-rate works. Touches on jazz in the fiction of Chandler Brossard, Bernard Wolfe, Terry Southern, Rudolph Fisher, and J. D. Salinger. Finishes with complimentary comments about Josef Škvorecký's "The Bass Saxophone."

372. Tallman, Warren. "Kerouac's Sound." *Evergreen Review* 4.11 (Jan.-Feb. 1960): 153-169.

—. —. *A Casebook on the Beat.* Ed. Thomas Parkinson. New York: Crowell, 1961. 215-229.

Though Jack Kerouac is not regarded as a writer of jazz novels, jazz had such a strong influence on his writing that his spontaneous prose style has often been likened to the jazz improvisation of a bop musician. This piece, one of the earliest scholarly essays on Kerouac, examines the influence of jazz on Kerouac's prose in *The Town and the City, On the Road, The Subterraneans,* and *The Dharma Bums.*

373. Taylor, Billy. "Jazz: America's Classical Music." *The Black Perspective in Music* 14.1 (Winter 1986): 21-25.

Dr. William "Billy" Taylor, highly respected jazz pianist, jazz teacher, and jazz historian, gives an overview of what jazz is and what its place is in relation to the western-European classical music tradition, noting that though jazz "is based on an Afro-American value system . . . the music has transcended ethnic boundaries and reflects and defines the national character as well as the national culture" (24).

374. Thomas, Leroy. "Welty's 'Powerhouse.'" *Explicator* 36.4 (Summer 1978): 15-17.

Thomas says "Powerhouse" emphasizes the theme of alienation on various levels: the alienation of Powerhouse as a black and as a musician, and the alienation of various band members.

375. Tracy, Steven C. "Simple's Great African-American Joke." *CLA Journal* 27.3 (March 1984): 239-253.

Tracy discusses Langston Hughes's affirmation of "African beauty" and his raising black culture to a higher level of importance. "Very often to understand [Hughes's] work one must know blues and jazz in particular" (242). Jazz in "Jazz, Jive, and Jam" is regarded as low culture by Simple's wife, Joyce, and by Dr. Conboy. The story "advocates collective involvement to solve racial problems, through the creative interaction of leaders (purveyors of culture . . .) and the integrated participation of followers" (253). Hughes believed that African Americans needed to retain their cultural identity.

376. Traylor, Eleanor W. "Music as Theme: The Jazz Mode in the Works of Toni Cade Bambara." *Black Women Writers (1950-1980): A Critical Evaluation.* Ed. Mari Evans. Garden City, NY: Anchor-Doubleday, 1984. 58-70.

Concentrates on *The Salt Eaters*, calling it "a modern myth of creation told in the jazz mode" (59). "The improvising, stylizing, vamping, re-creative method of the jazz composer is the formal method by which the narrative genius of Toni Cade Bambara evokes a usable past testing its values within an examined present moment while simultaneously exploring the re-creative and transformative possibilities of experience. The method of the jazz composition informs the central themes and large revelation of the world of Bambara's fiction" (65).

377. Valentine, Robert Y. "The Creative Personality in Cortázar's 'El Perseguidor.'" *Journal of Spanish Studies* 2.3 (Winter 1974): 169-191.

Maintains that Cortázar is examining himself through the character of Johnny, the jazz saxophonist modeled on Charlie Parker, and through the jazz critic, Bruno. "An intellectual, [Cortázar] exemplifies many of Bruno's traits. And, like Johnny, an expatriot from America, he seeks his own voice by transcending the conventional limitations of his art form, to do with language what the jazzman does with music" (186). Valentine feels that "Cortázar's personality is a composite of the creator or visionary and the critic or aesthetician" (186).

378. Walcott, Ronald. "The Early Fiction of John A. Williams." *CLA Journal* 16 (1972): 198-213.

Examines some of the autobiographical roots of Williams's work in *The Angry Ones, Sissie,* and *Night Song.* Walcott judges *Night Song* to be "barely a competent [novel]" (207) because its characters never really come alive. He sees the novel centering on Keel Robinson's need to come to terms with his racial identity and regards the central jazz figure, Richie "Eagle" Stokes, as representative of the "tragic black genius" (205).

379. Watson, Edward A. "Bessie's Blues." *New Letters* 38, No. 2 (Winter 1971): 64-70.

—. —. *Bigger Thomas.* Ed. Harold Bloom. New York: Chelsea House, 1990. 54-59.

Watson feels that Richard Wright in *Native Son* makes a subtle blues reference through Bigger's girl friend, Bessie Mears. He reconstructs her laments as blues lyrics that "correspond with, and form a counterpoint to the three divisions of the book—Fear, Flight, Fate" (57).

380. Wegs, Joyce M. "Toni Morrison's *Song of Solomon.*" *Essays in Literature* 9 (Fall 1982): 211-223.

A number of African-American writers have used the blues form and content in a structural way. Here Joyce M. Wegs discusses men as "flyers" who run away from problems and women as "singers" of blues, lamenters. Her essay "[explores] how Morrison seeks in fiction to enliven and replenish the function music used to serve in its clarification of roles and its comparison of old and new values . . . [and demonstrates] how Morrison as novelist takes on the role of a blues singer in order both to explore how folk values buried in the past may contribute to a better future for all her people and to describe variations on traditional male and female roles in order that her readers may analyze for themselves which ones appear most valuable" (211-212).

381. Weiner, Marc A. "*Urwaldmusik* and the Borders of German Identity: Jazz in Literature of the Weimar Republic." *The German Quarterly* 64.4 (1991): 475-487.

Discusses the reception of jazz in Germany from 1920 to about 1933. Weiner's essay "analyzes the ideological function(s) of jazz attending its appearance in diverse literary and extraliterary texts of the Weimar Republic and . . . seeks to demonstrate how such music provided a locus for the expression of extramusical concerns in German society at the time" (475). Works looked at in some detail are Vicki Baum's *Stud. chem Helene Willfür,* Herman Hesse's *Der Steppenwolf,* Bruno Frank's *Politische Novelle,* René Schickele's *Symphonie für Jazz,* and Klaus Mann's *Mephisto.*

382. West, Ray B., Jr. "Three Methods of Modern Fiction: Ernest Hemingway, Thomas Mann, Eudora Welty." *College English* 12.4 (January 1951): 193-203.

In Section III, "Theme Through Symbol," West discusses Welty's "Powerhouse." He says that Welty expresses her theme using "the technique of the musician" (199). He says the relationship between Power-house and his musicians ranges "from mysticism to cynicism" and that "their instruments depict similar relationships to Powerhouse's piano" (200). "The subject matter of "Powerhouse" is the relationship between fiction and fact, and the story delineates through the intricate weaving of the symbolic themes their highest relationship as symbolized in the man of primitive genius, Powerhouse: his relationship to members of his orchestra, to members of his race, and to all mankind" (201).

383. Westerath, Gerhard. "Pynchon's Parker Passage." *Pynchon Notes* 20-21 (Spring-Fall 1987):109-114.

Beyond Kerouac and the Beats, the great impact of jazz on a variety of writers in the 1950s is further seen in Thomas Pynchon. His allusions to jazz icons are seen in both *V.*, where Thelonious Monk is the model for McClintic Sphere, and in *Gravity's Rainbow*, where the prominent jazz allusion is to Charlie Parker. Westerath says that "Pynchon writes with an essential awareness of the acoustic quality of all writing" (110) and that he "clearly projects his admiration for the virtuosity and musicality of Parker's playing, and by means of changing perspectives he allows the reader to share the experience directly" (111).

384. Weyl, Donald M. "The Vision of Man in the Novels of William Melvin Kelley." *Critique* 15.3 (1973): 15-33.

Discusses *A Different Drummer*, *Dancers on the Shore*, *A Drop of Patience*, and *dem*. Sees Ludlow, the black blind jazz musician in *A Drop of Patience*, as a man in search of his identity who finds that communion between blacks and whites is improbable because of the fear that whites have of blacks.

385. Wilkerson, Margaret B. "Music as Metaphor: New Plays of Black Women." *Making a Spectacle: Feminist Essays on Contemporary Women's Theatre*. Ed. Lynda Hunt. Ann Arbor: U Michigan P, 1989. 61-75.

Wilkerson says that "contemporary black women playwrights find in music a second language that gives expression to the profound anguish and joy of their vision and experience" (62). She devotes most of her discussion to Alexis DeVeaux's *The Tapestry*, Aishah Rahman's *Unfinished Women Cry in No Man's Land While a Bird Dies in a Gilded Cage*, and P. J. Gibson's *Brown Silk and Magenta Sunsets*, all of which involve jazz musicians as important characters. She gives emphasis to Rahman's use of Charlie

Parker and that in all of these three plays there are female characters who are seduced by the music of jazz men.

386. Williams, Shirley Anne. "The Black Musician: The Black Hero as Light Bearer." *Give Birth to Brightness*. New York: Dial, 1972. 135-166.

Emphasizes the importance of Black music as "the chief artifact created out of the Black experience" but notes that the music and musicians "are generally touched upon lightly and rarely explored as a theme deserving of individual and primary treatment," but rather "with a hedonistic, often raffish, sometimes shiftless, way of life which is in conflict with or depicted in contrast to conventional morality and respectability." With references to Baldwin's "Sonny's Blues," *Another Country*, and *Blues for Mister Charlie*, Williams provides a more realistic account of the use of black music as metaphor and the black musician as one who deals in dreams and in love.

387. Wilson, Ann. "*Coming Through Slaughter*: Storyville Twice Told." *Descant* 14.4 (Fall 1983): 99-111.

Compares the novel and play versions of Michael Ondaatje's story. Concentrates on Buddy Bolden's tendency toward self-destruction and his various identities. Wilson says that Bolden's "life and his music were inseparable" (101) and that little is known of each. She discusses Bolden's relationship with the photographer Belloc and says he represents a balance in Bolden's life. In the novel, Ondaatje's connection to the character Bolden is evident, but in the theatrical version, the author is absent.

388. Young, Al, Larry Kart, and Michael S. Harper. "Jazz and Letters: A Colloquy." *TriQuarterly 68* (Winter 1987): 118-158.

Transcript of a panel discussion held in April 1986 at an annual meeting of the Associated Writing Programs. Jazz and literature are related to the ideas of freedom and spontaneity, especially in relation to the Beat Generation and Jack Kerouac.

INDEX OF NOVELS, PLAYS, AND SHORT STORIES

All numbers refer to bibliography numbers, the first being to the work itself and succeeding numbers to references to the works in critical articles.

GENERAL INDEX

All numbers following entries refer to item numbers in the bibliography.

About the Compiler

RICHARD N. ALBERT is Associate Professor Emeritus of English at Illinois State University. He has written extensively on the relationship between jazz and fiction, including *From Blues to Bop: A Collection of Jazz Fiction*, which he edited in 1990.